Test Color Page

Welcome to the fascinating world of "Zen Mandalas: Chromatic Therapy for Inner Peace".

In these pages, you will embark on a unique journey of self-discovery, relaxation and inspiration.

Mandalas, geometric shapes that represent the universe, become more than simple patterns - they become portals to tranquility.

Zen mandalas, known for their minimalist aesthetic and harmonious patterns, have been carefully selected to promote inner peace and serenity.

The journey is about to begin - may every stroke of color be a step towards your own serenity.

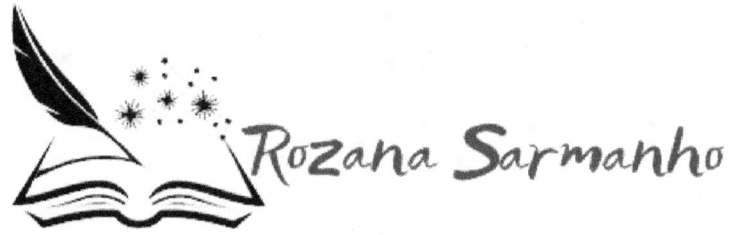

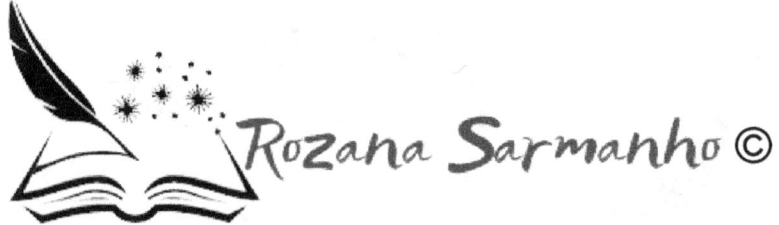

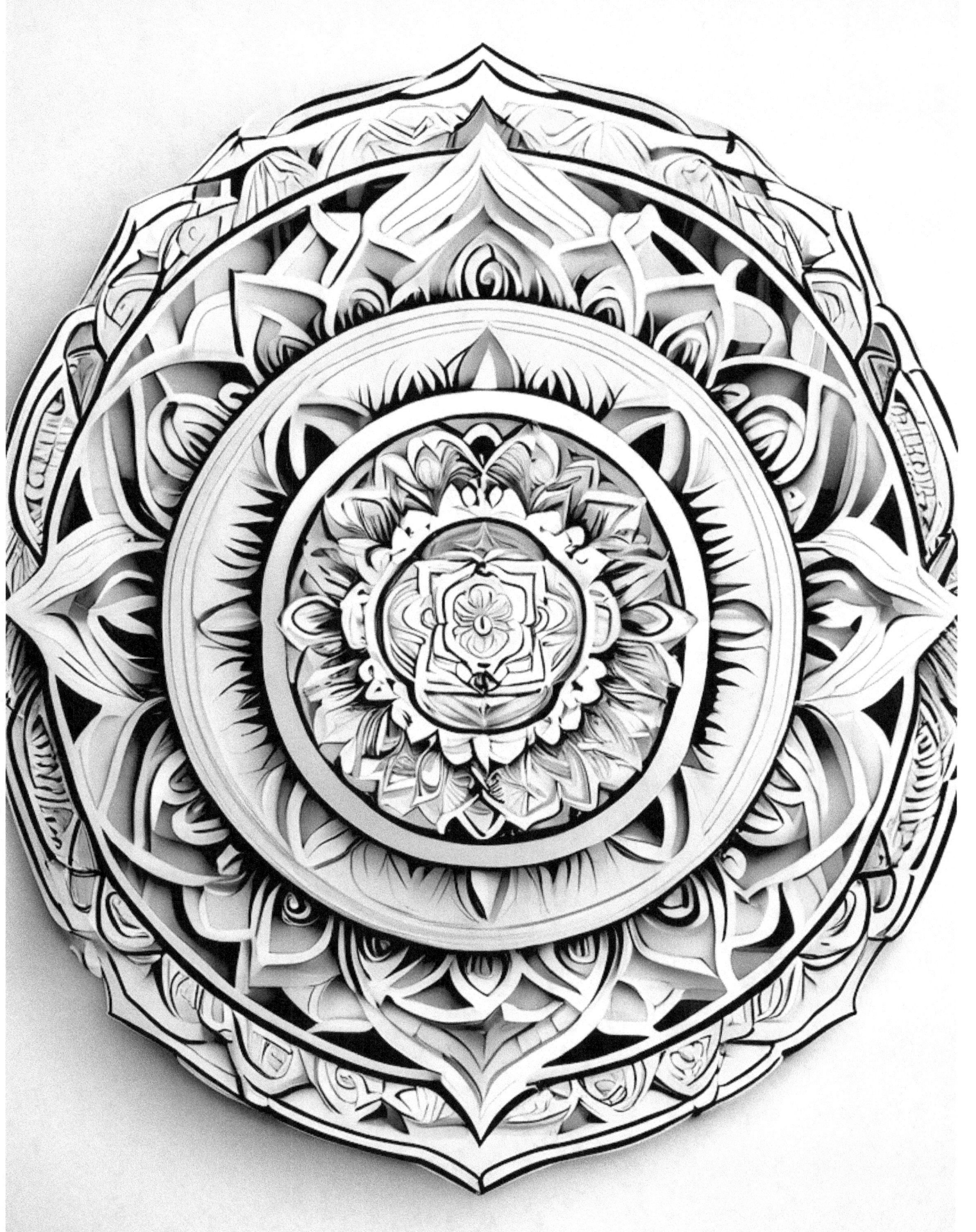

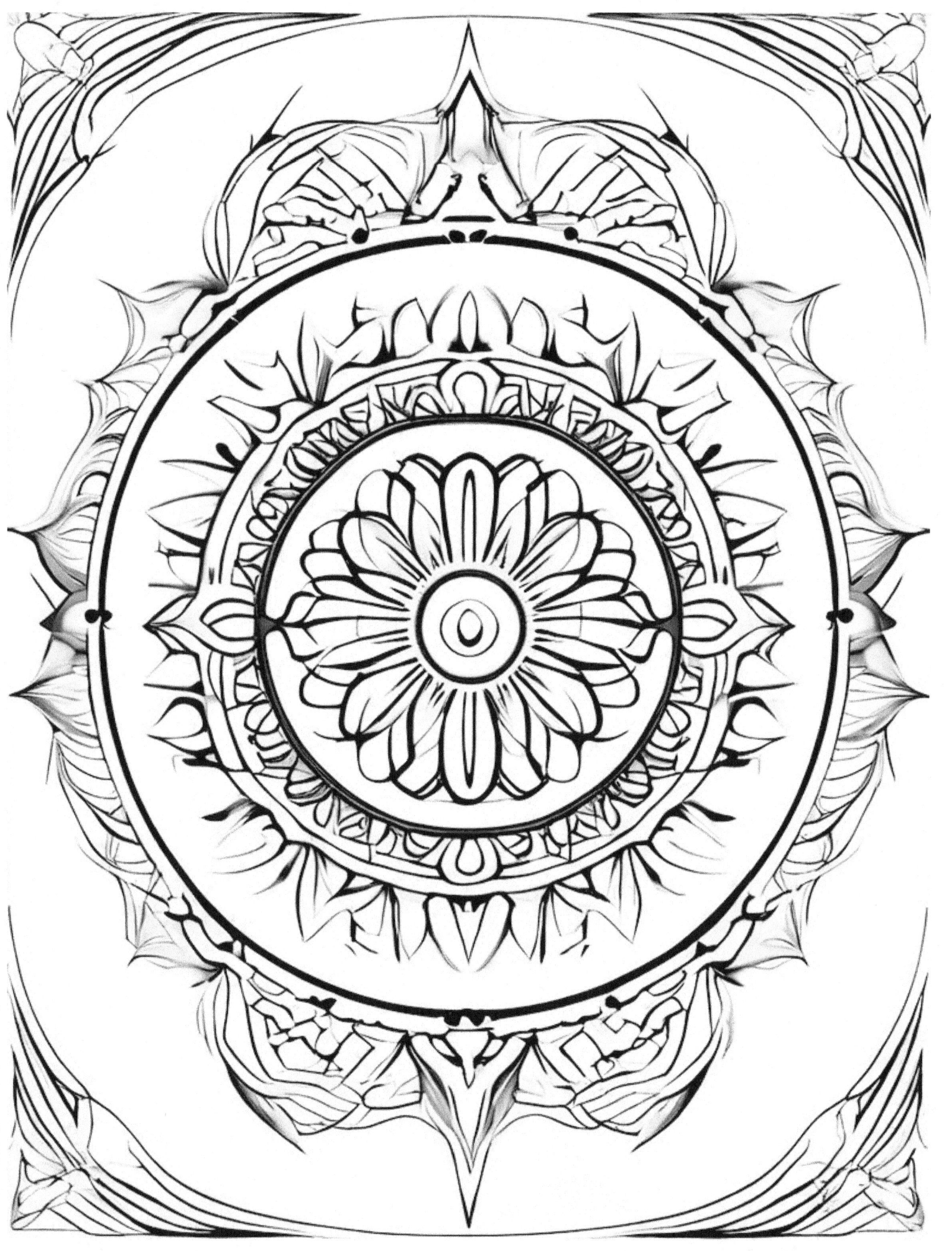

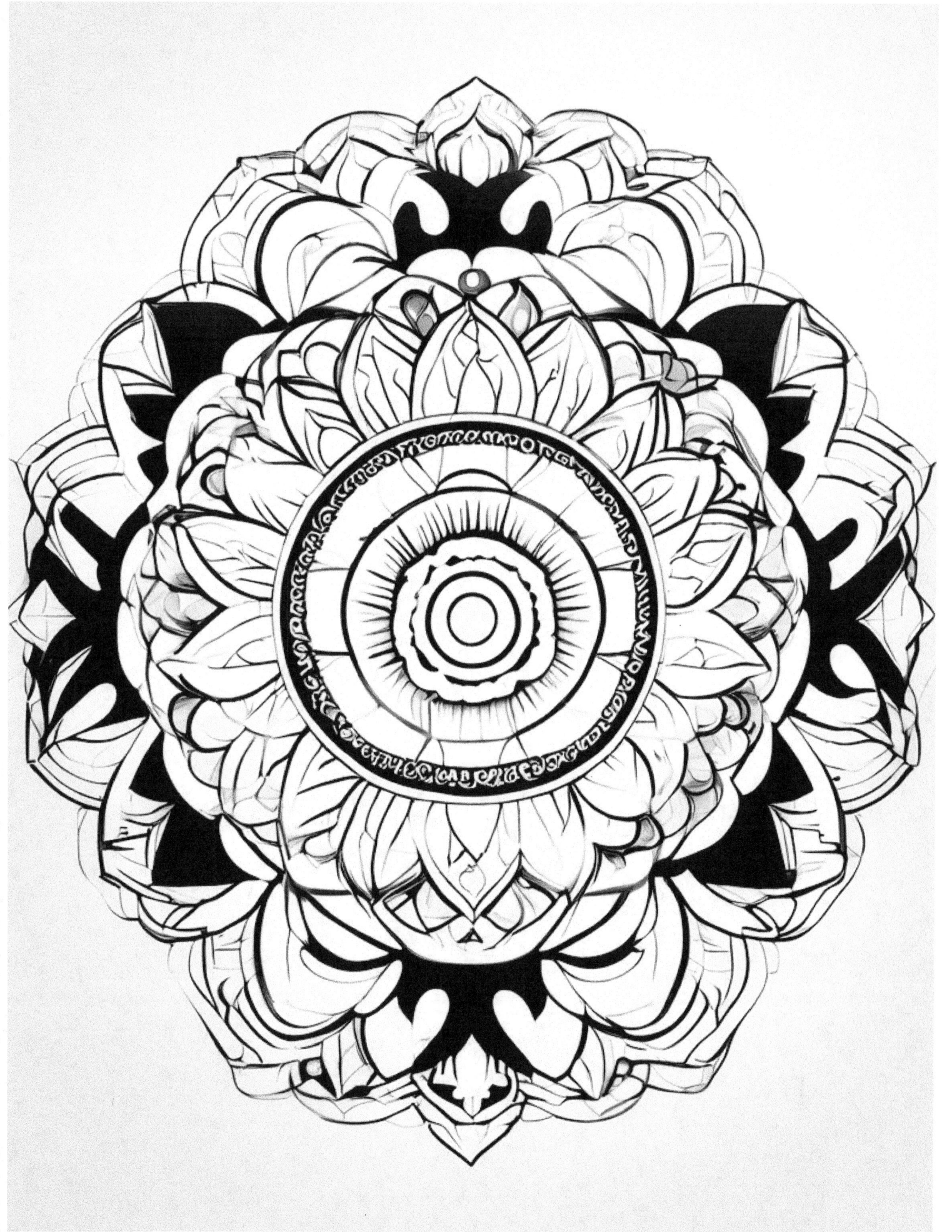

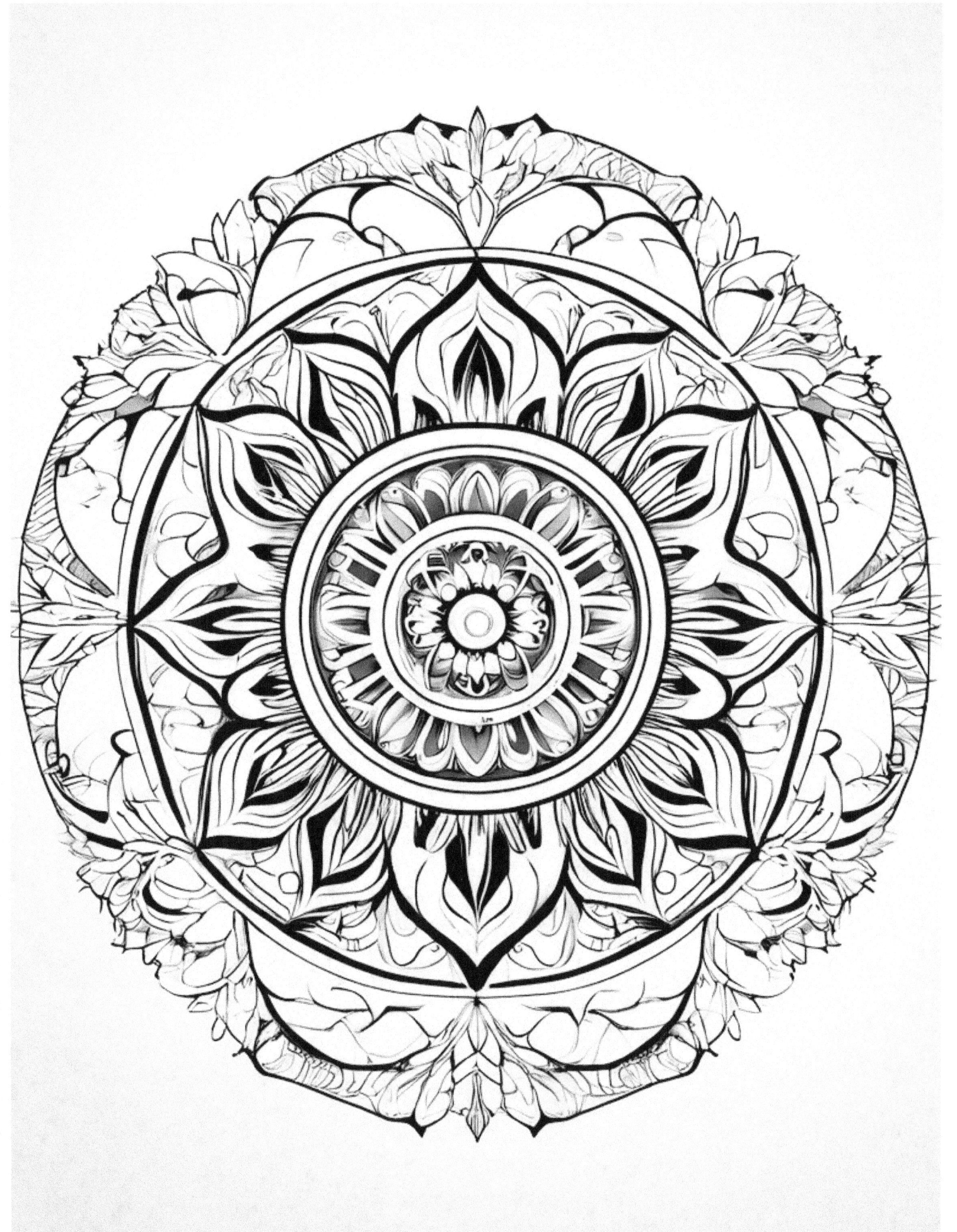

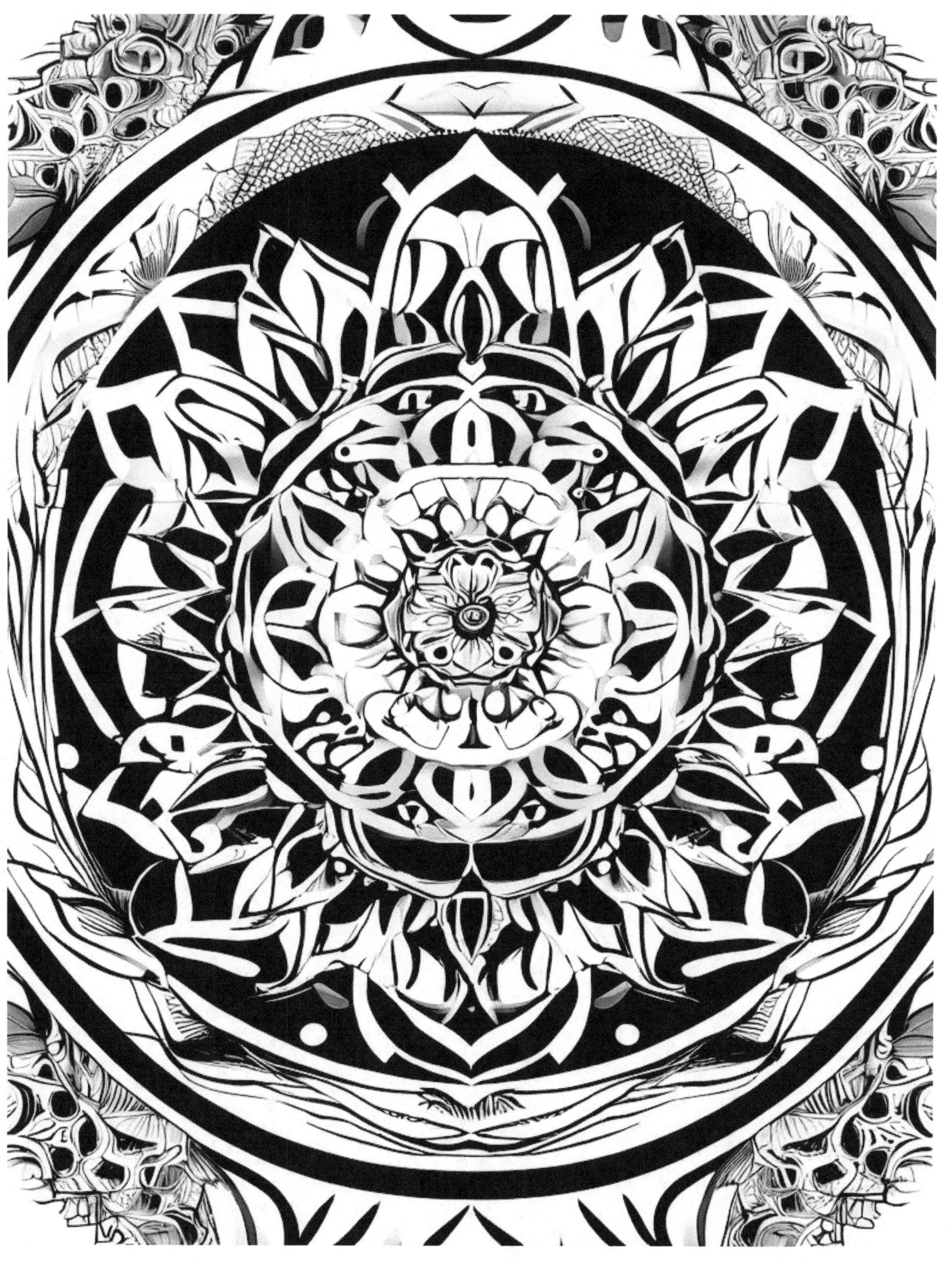

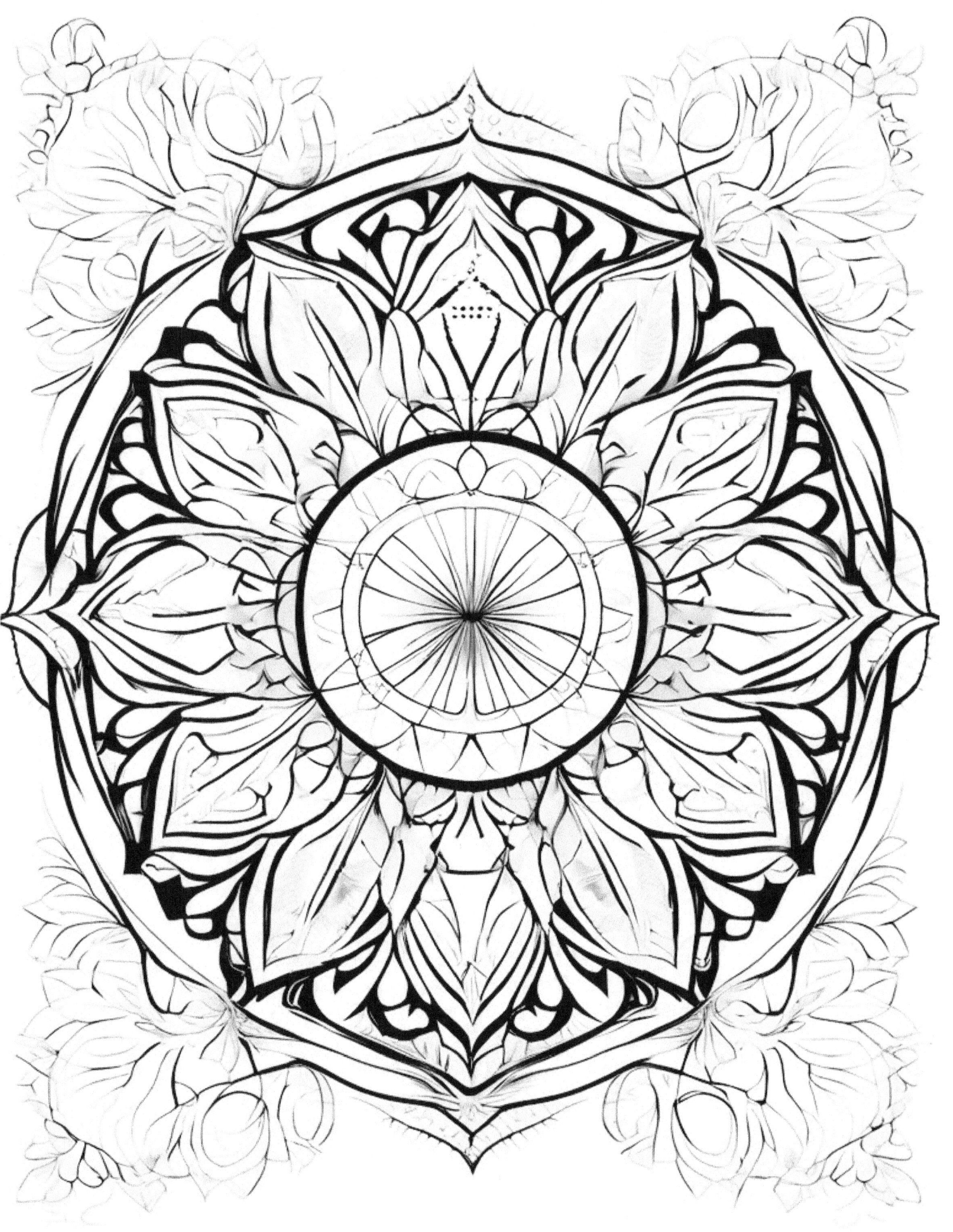

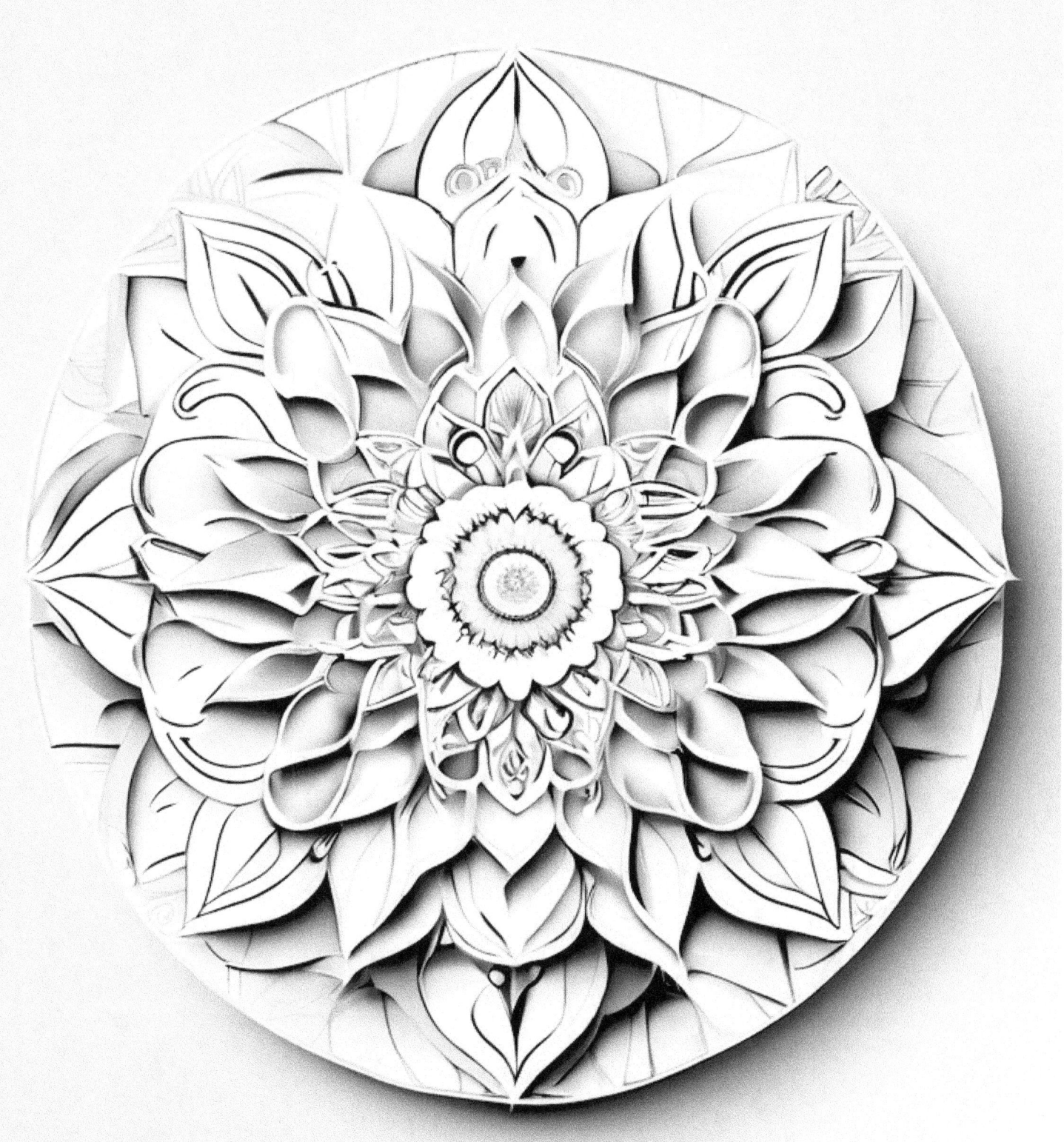

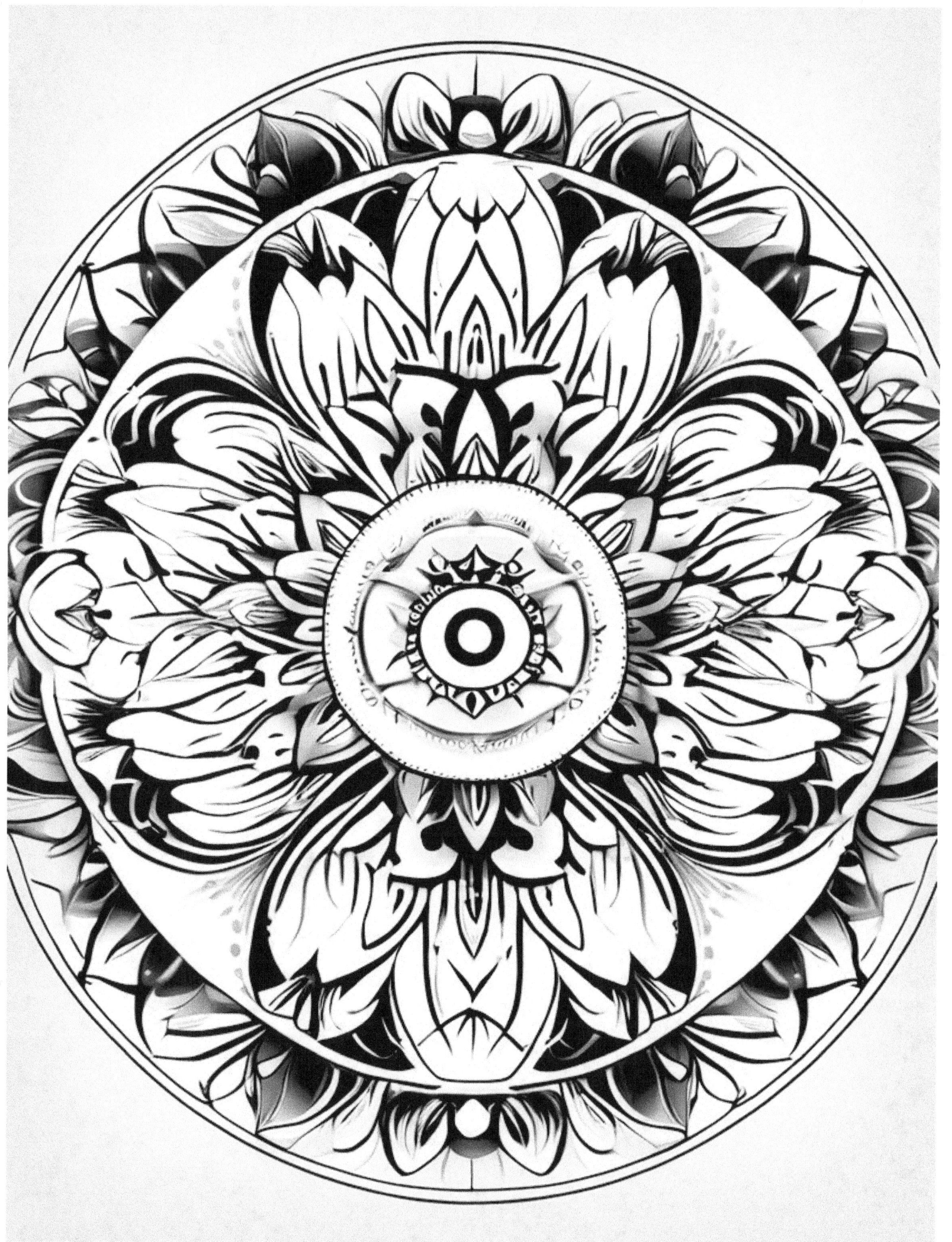

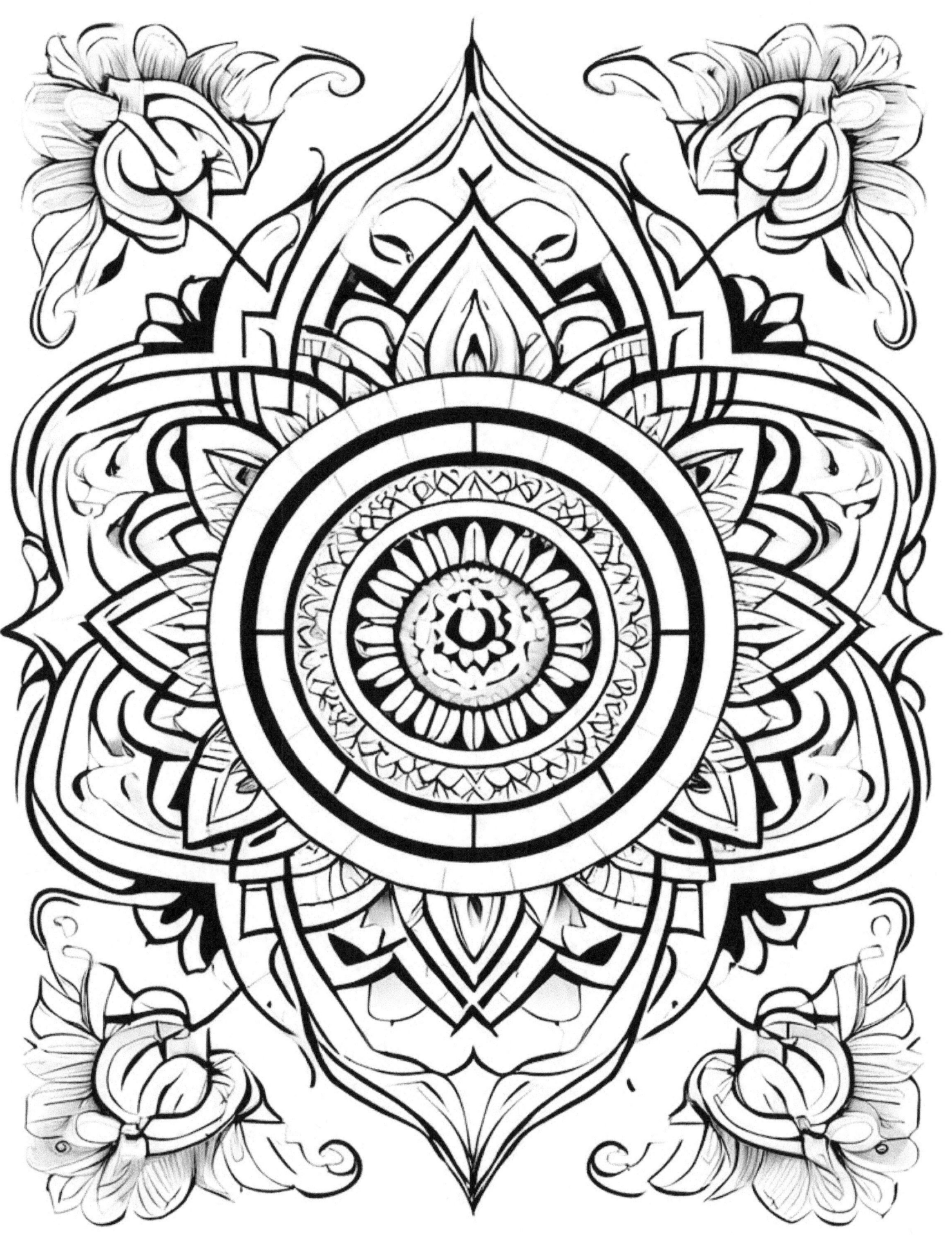

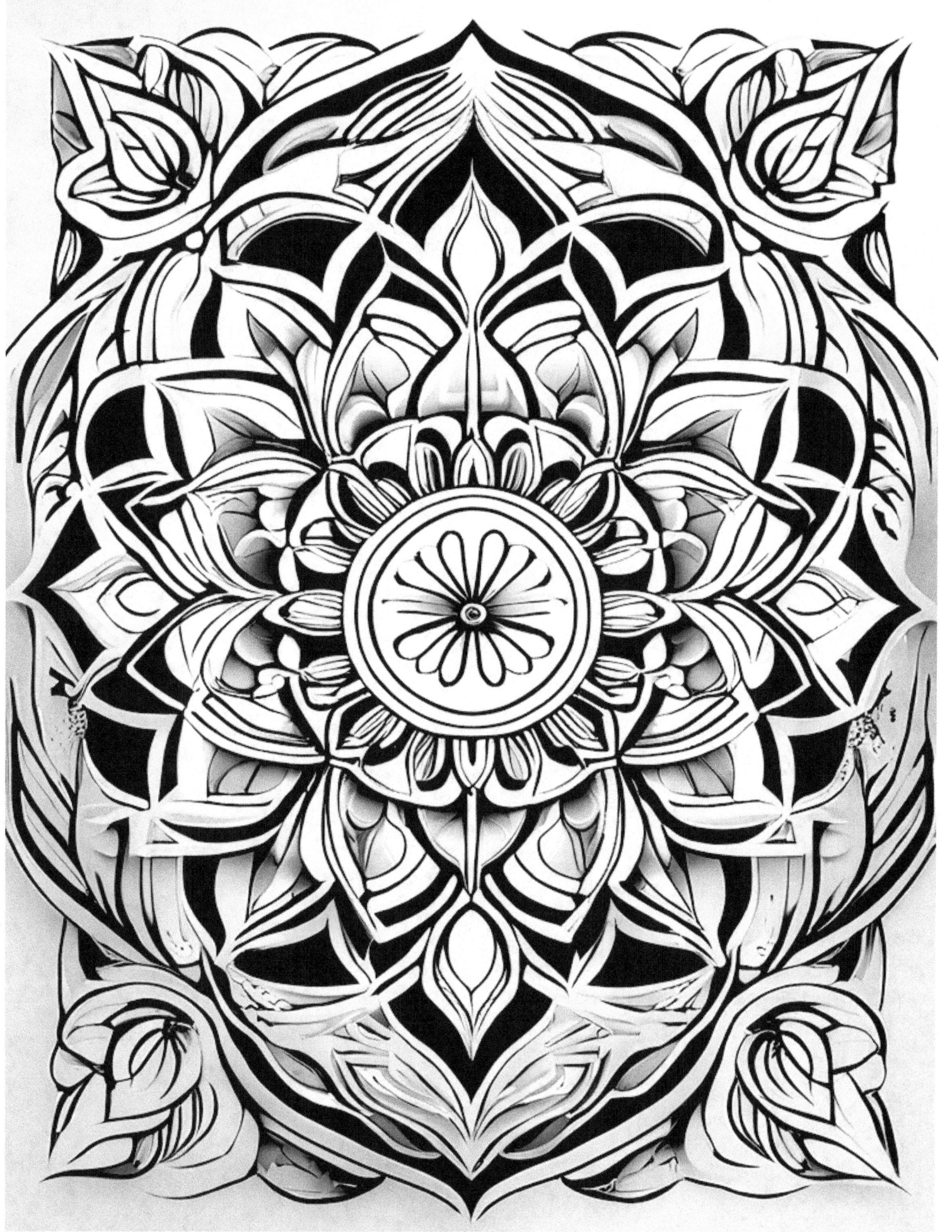

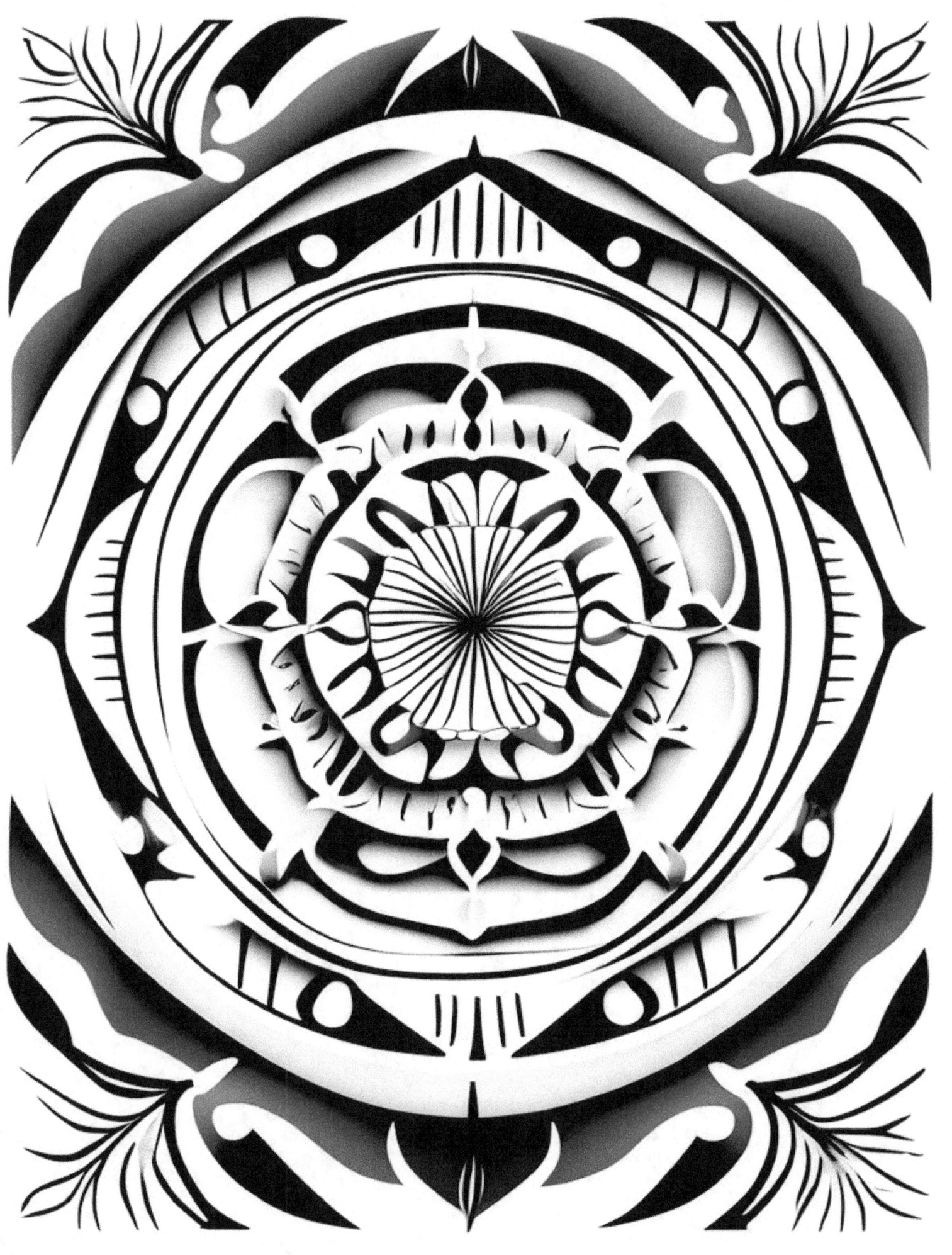

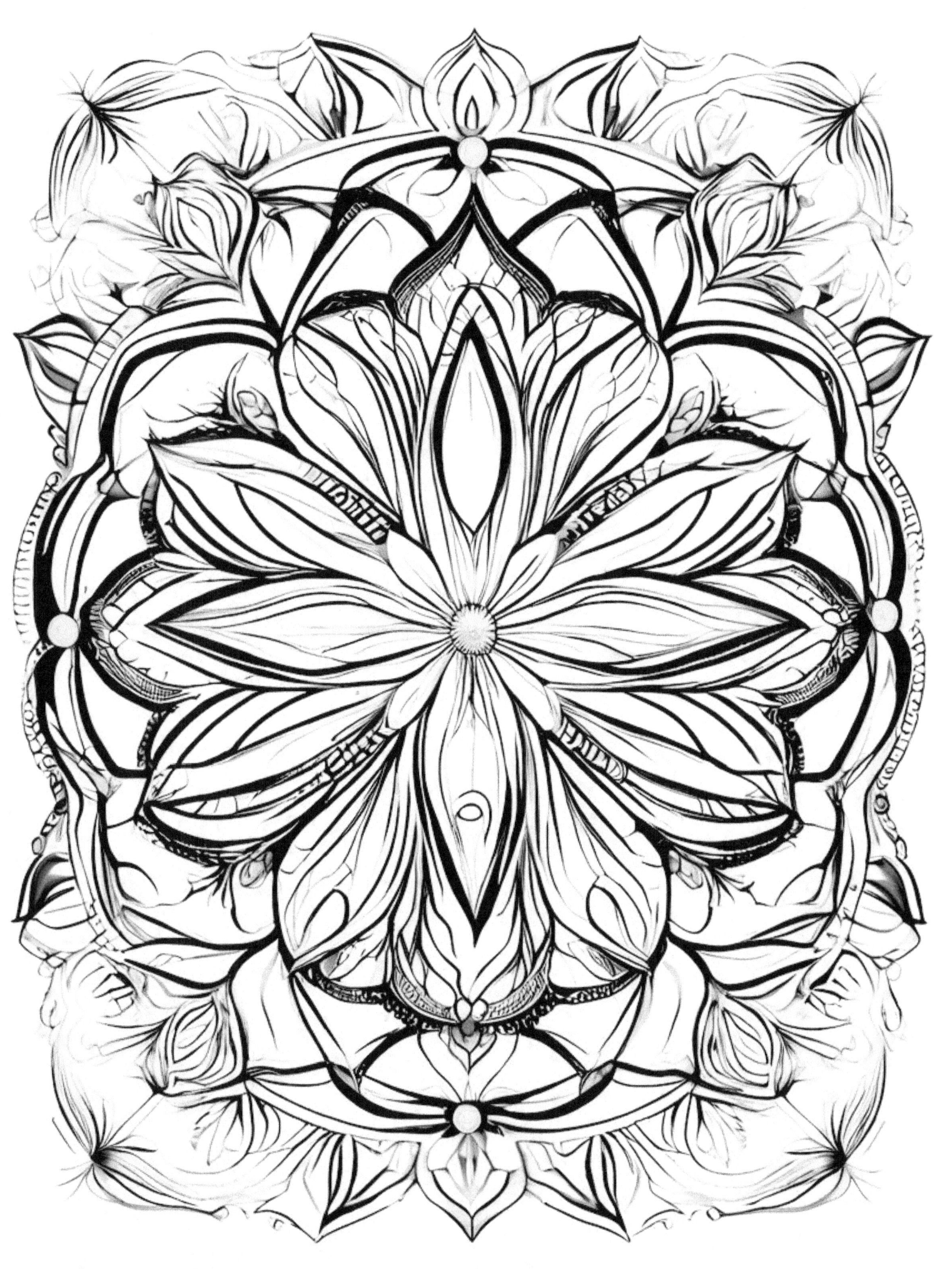

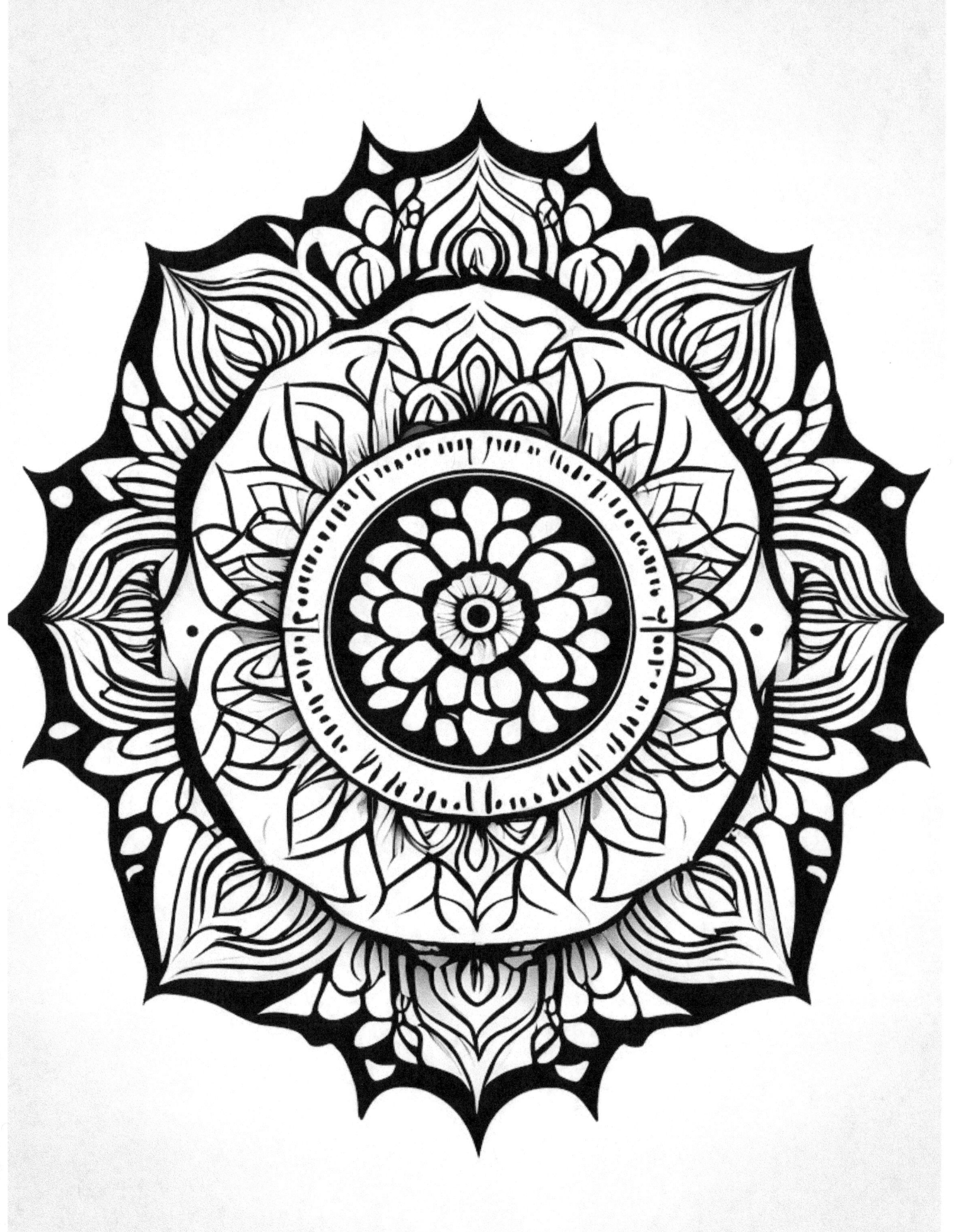

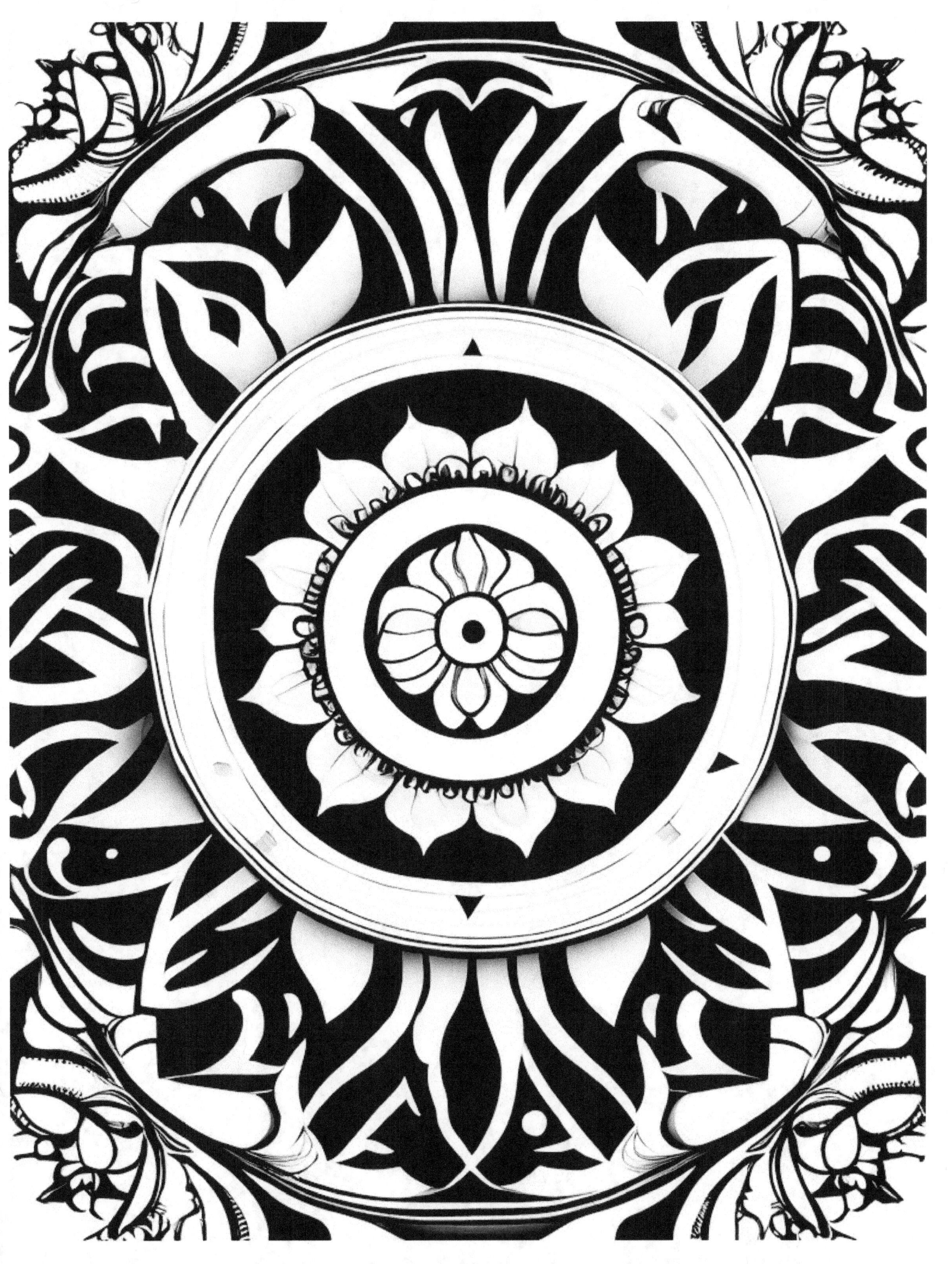

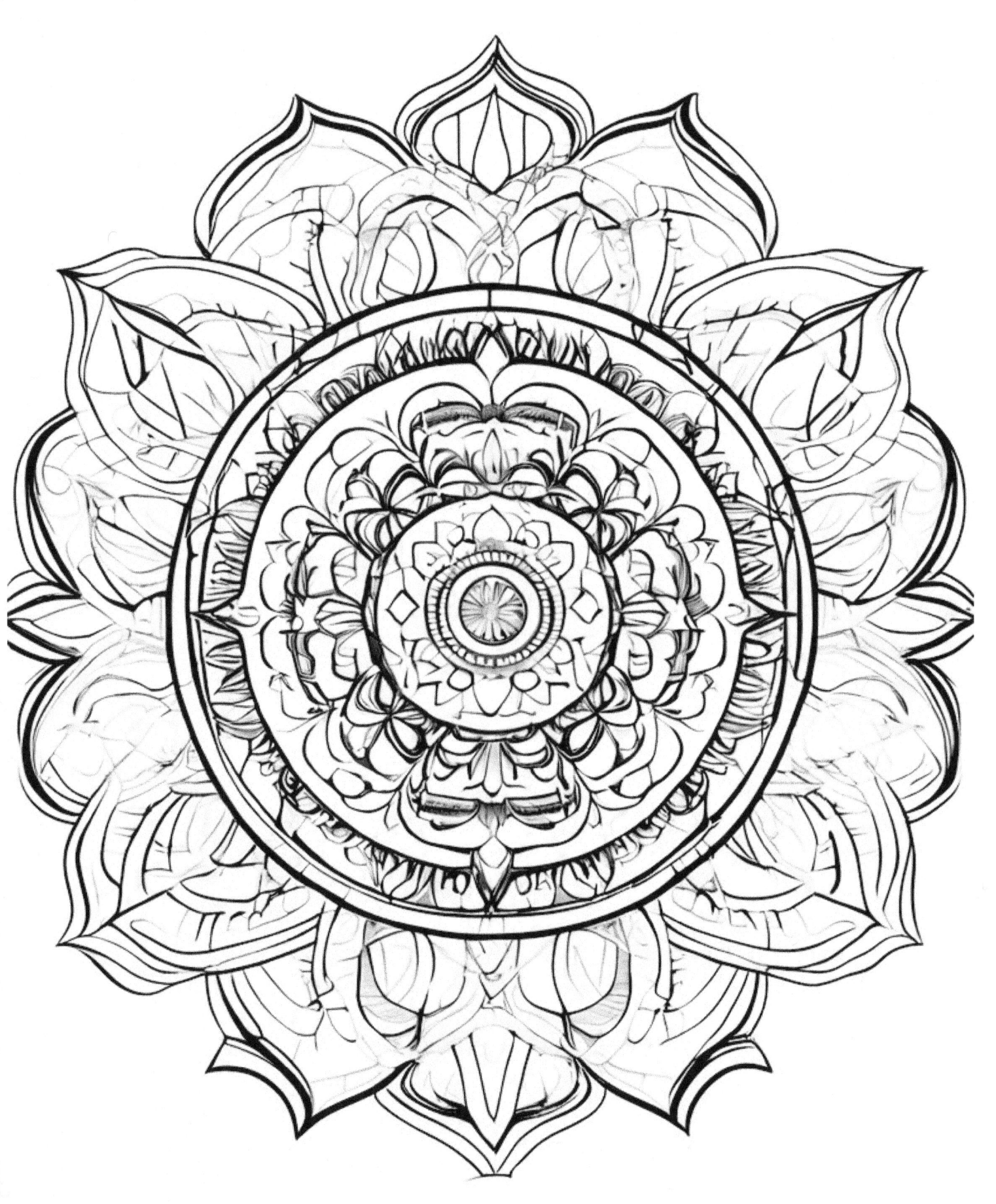

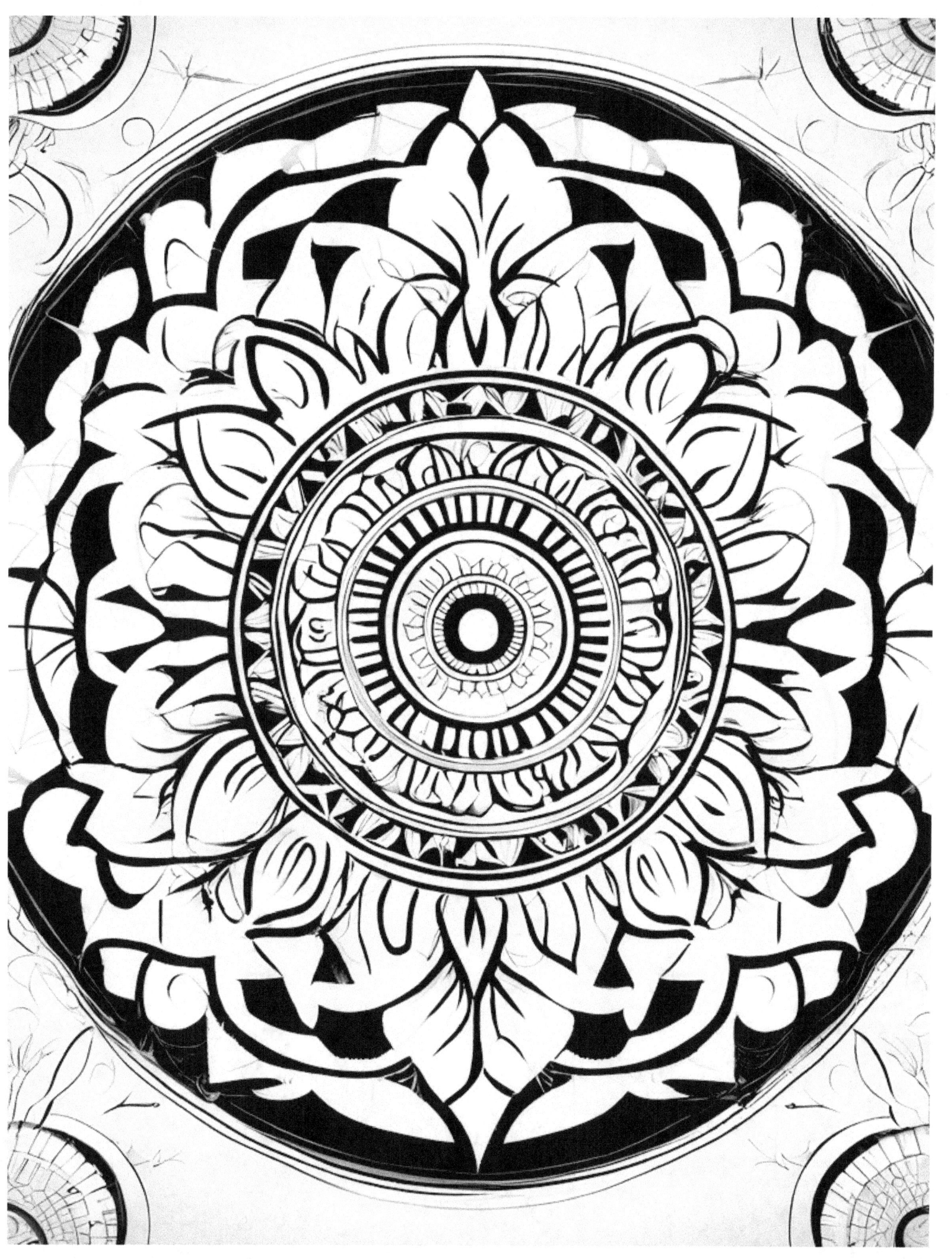

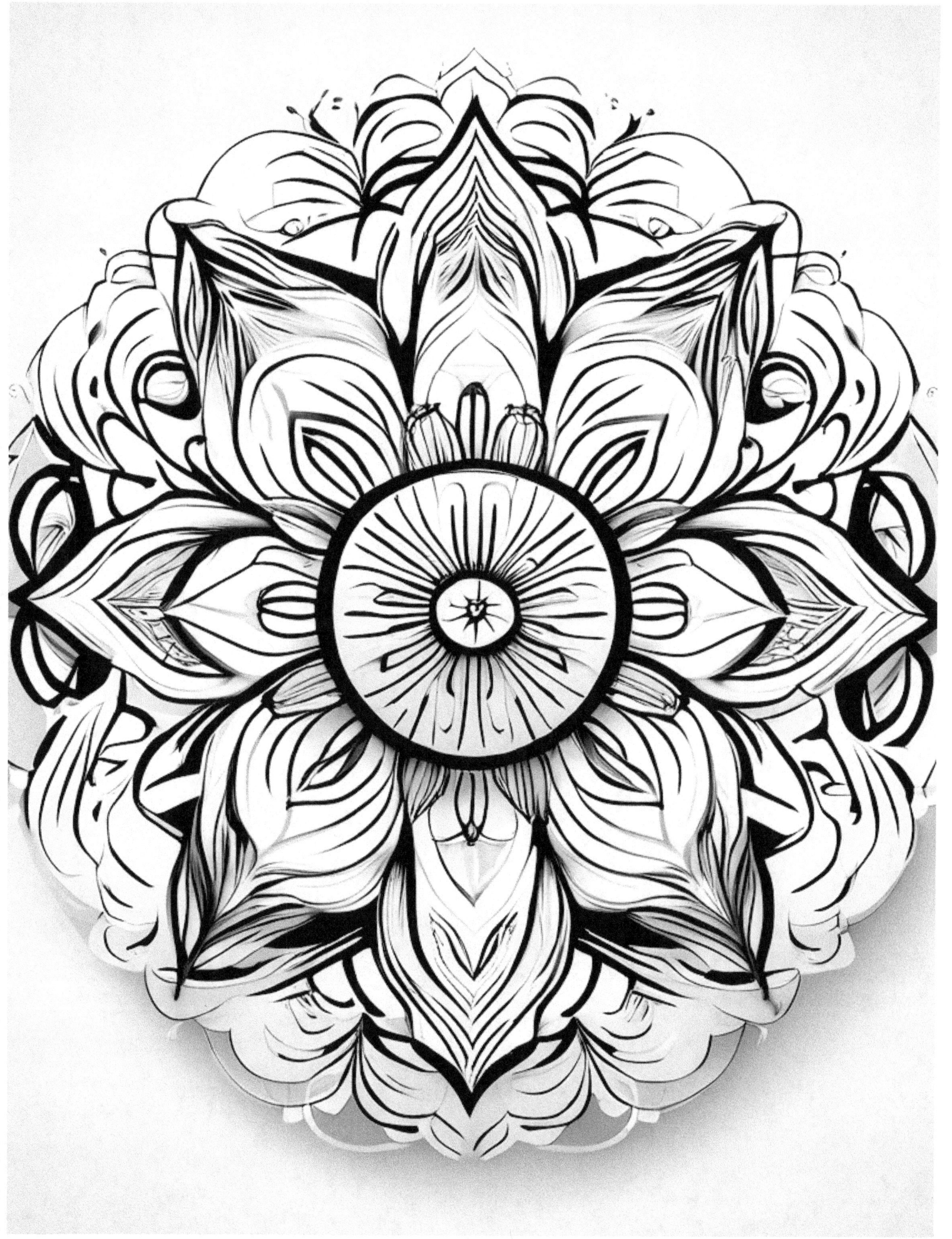

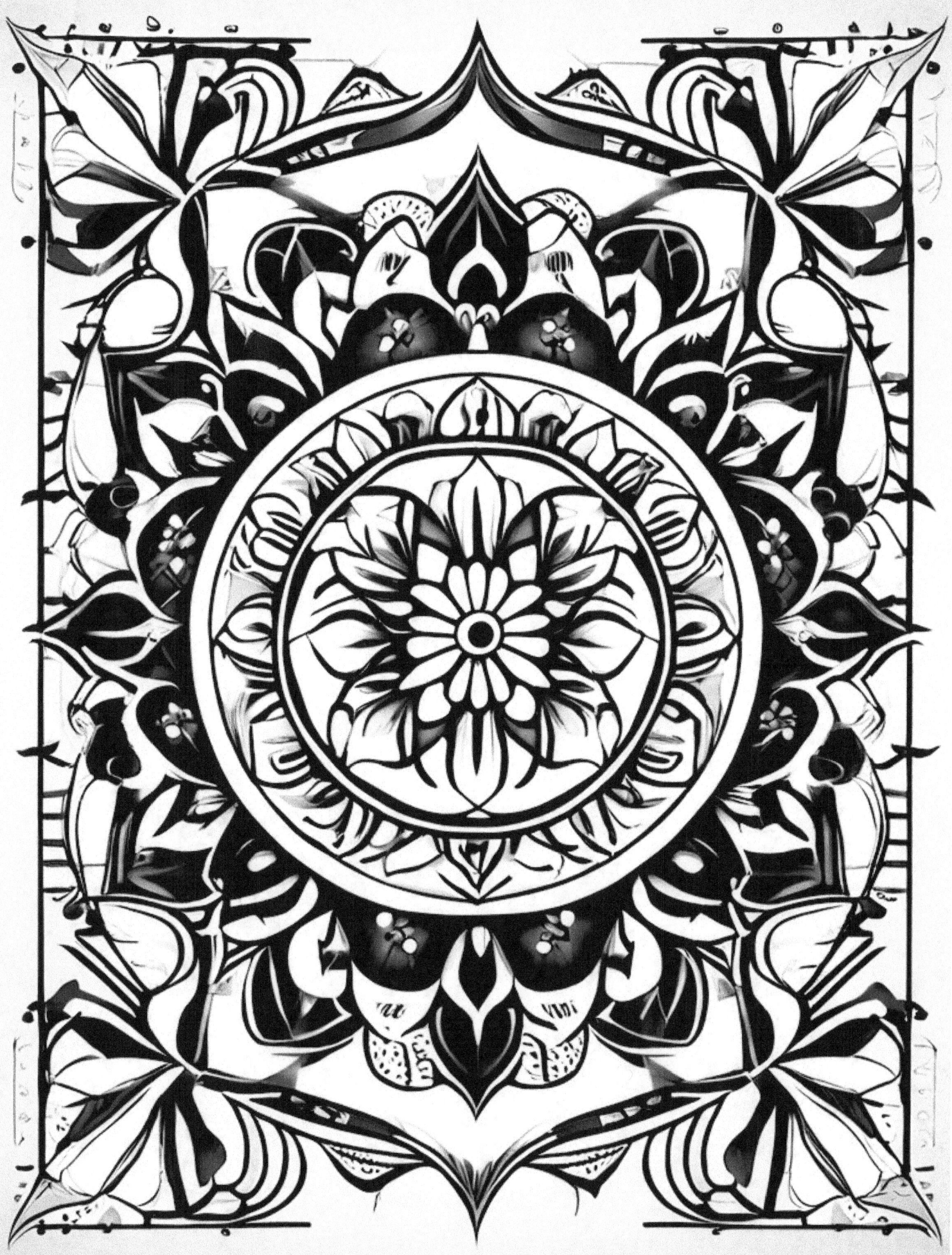

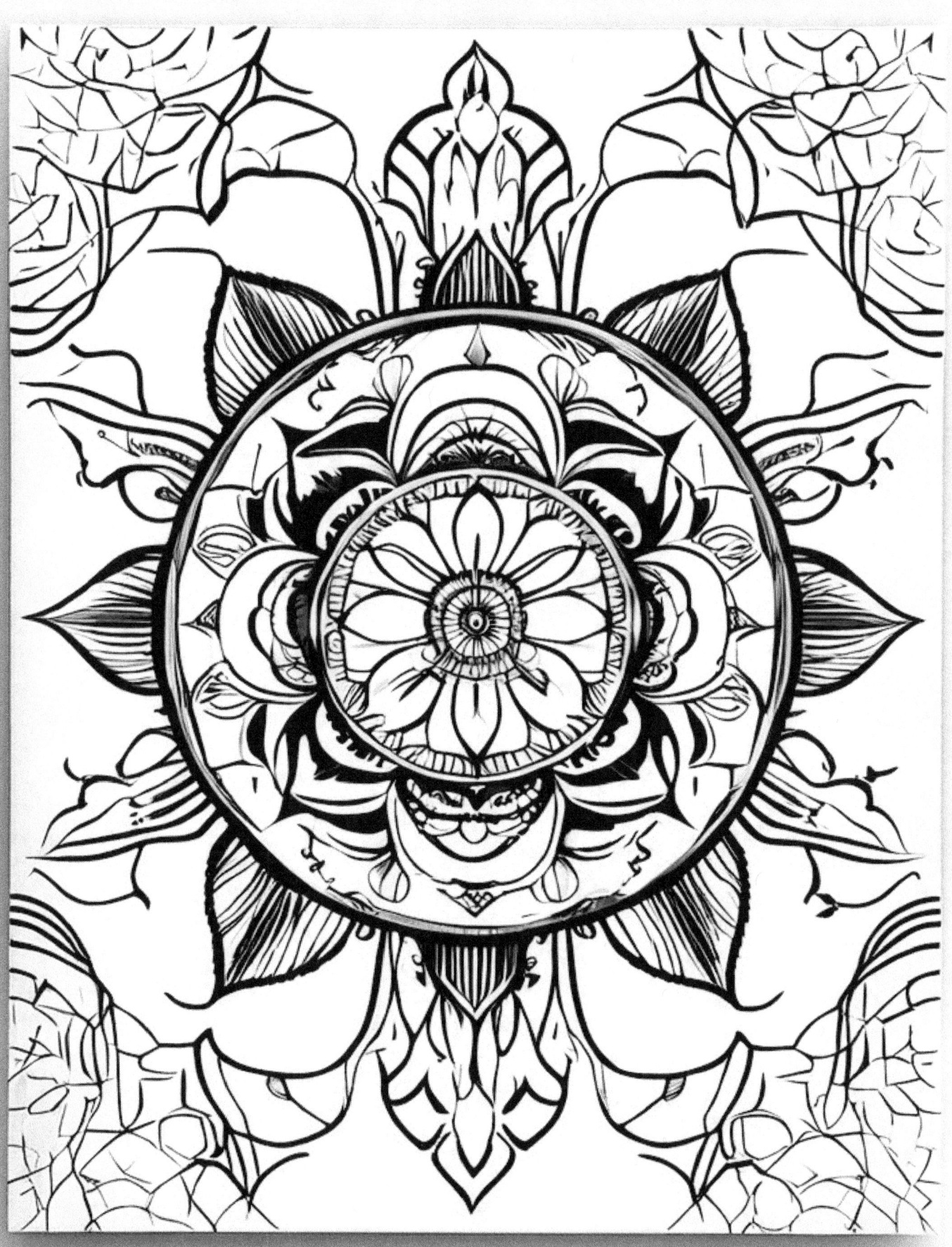

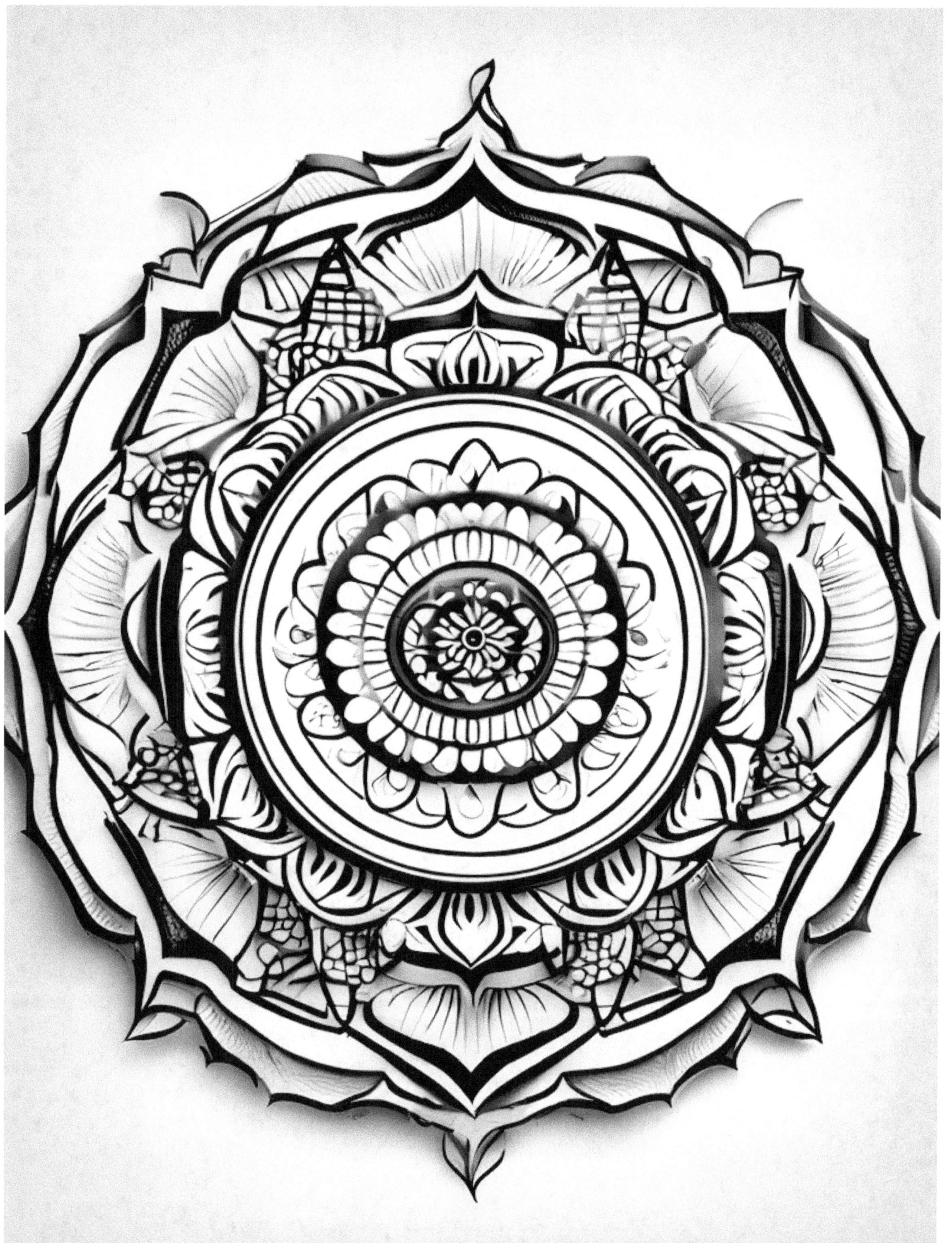

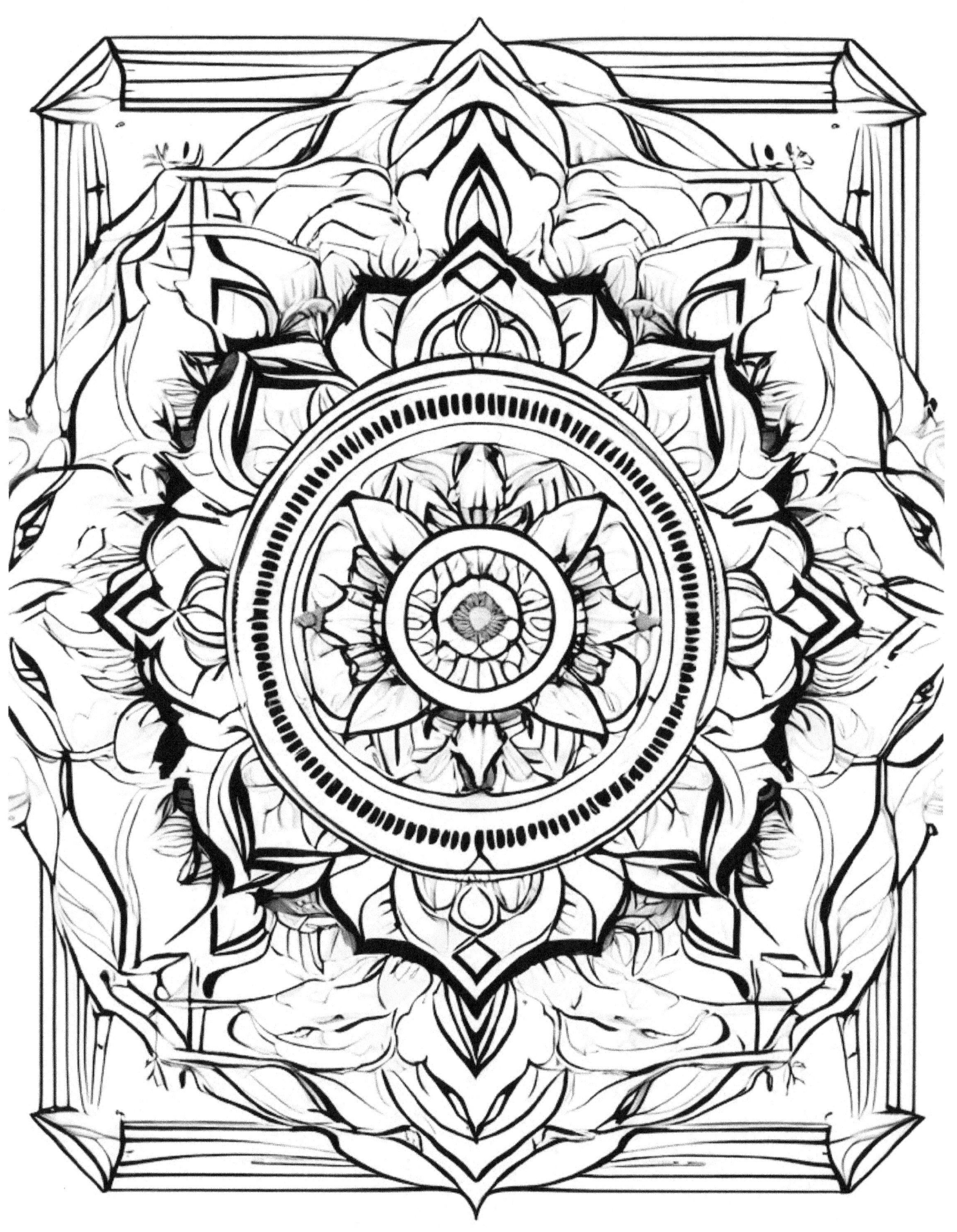

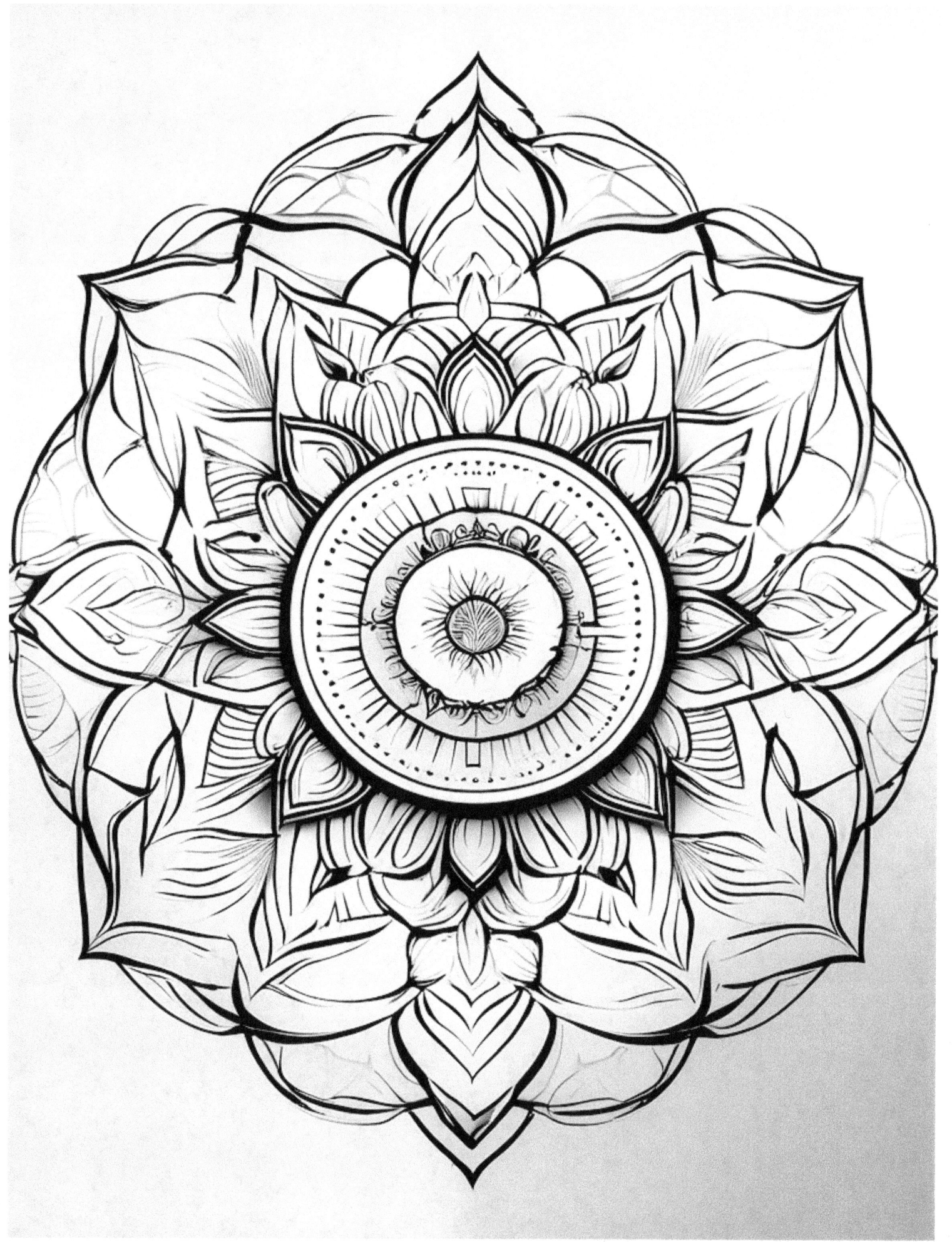

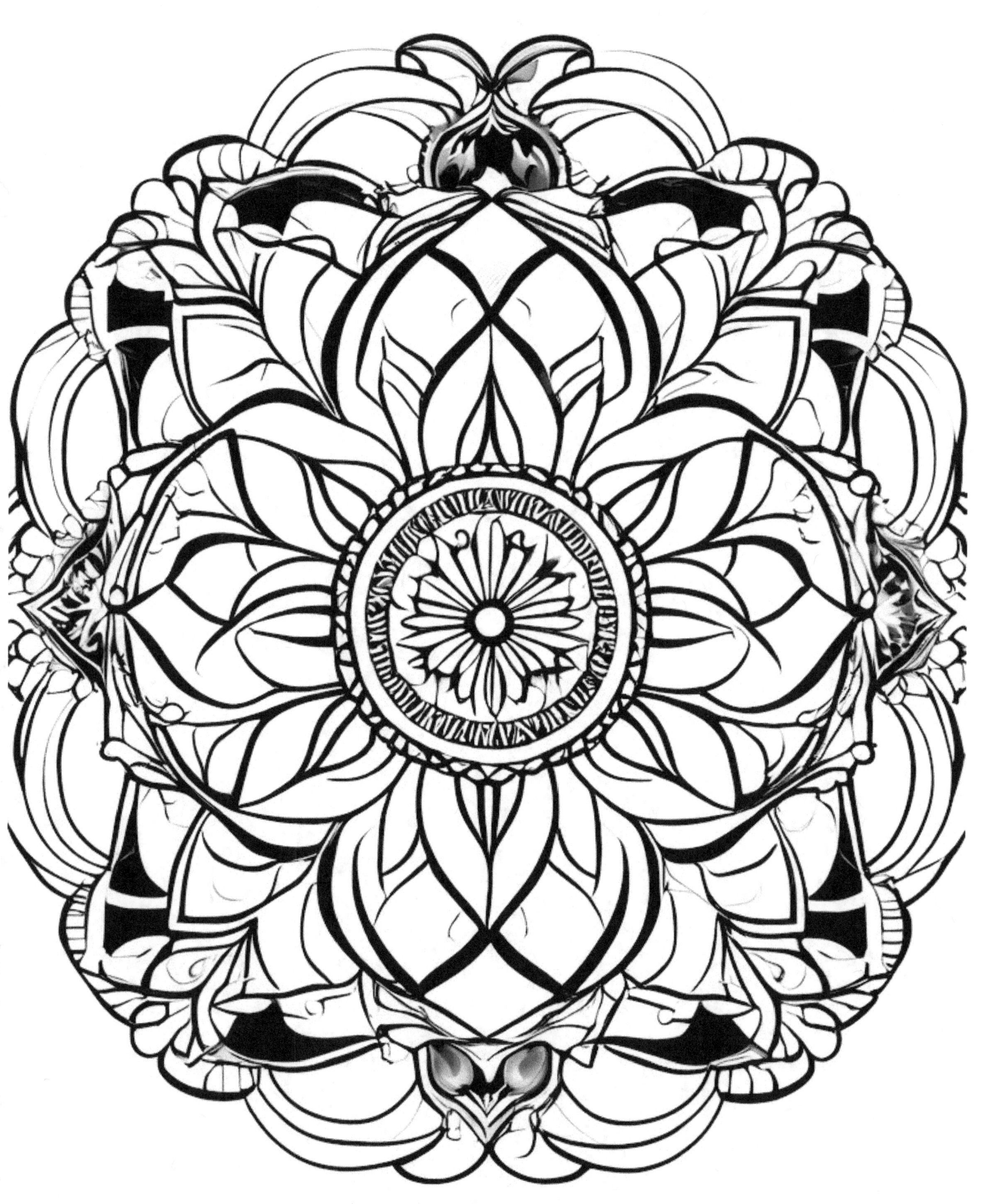

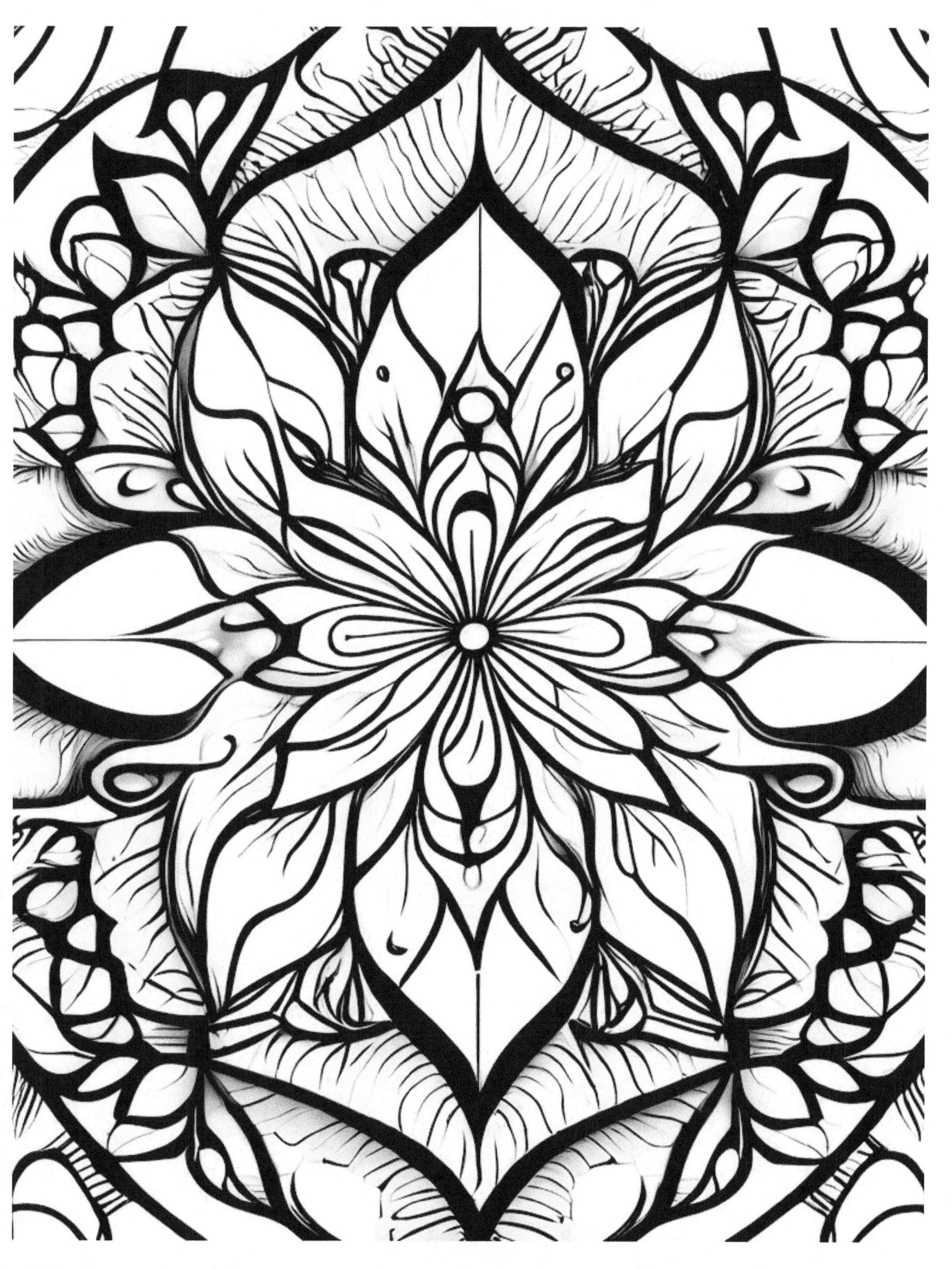

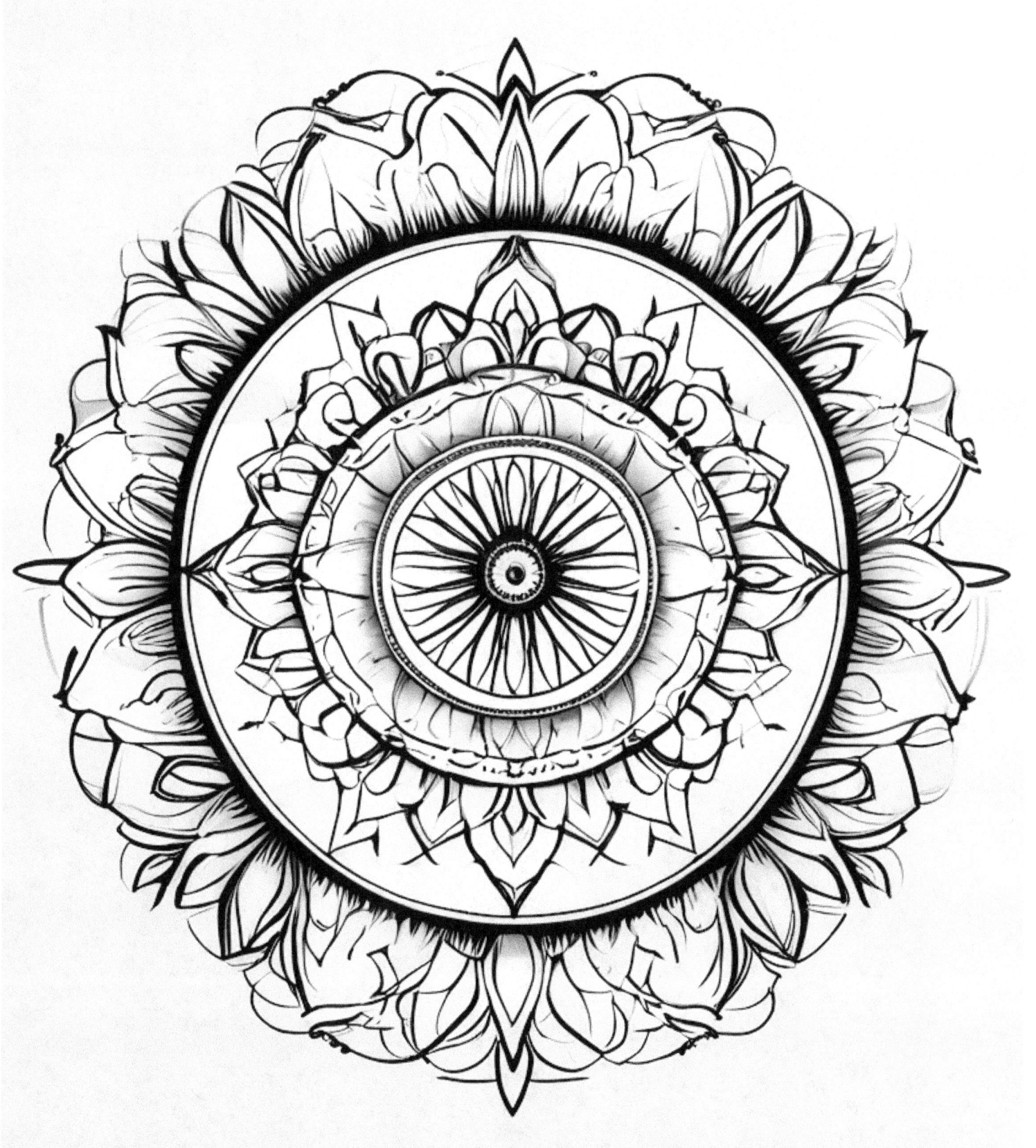

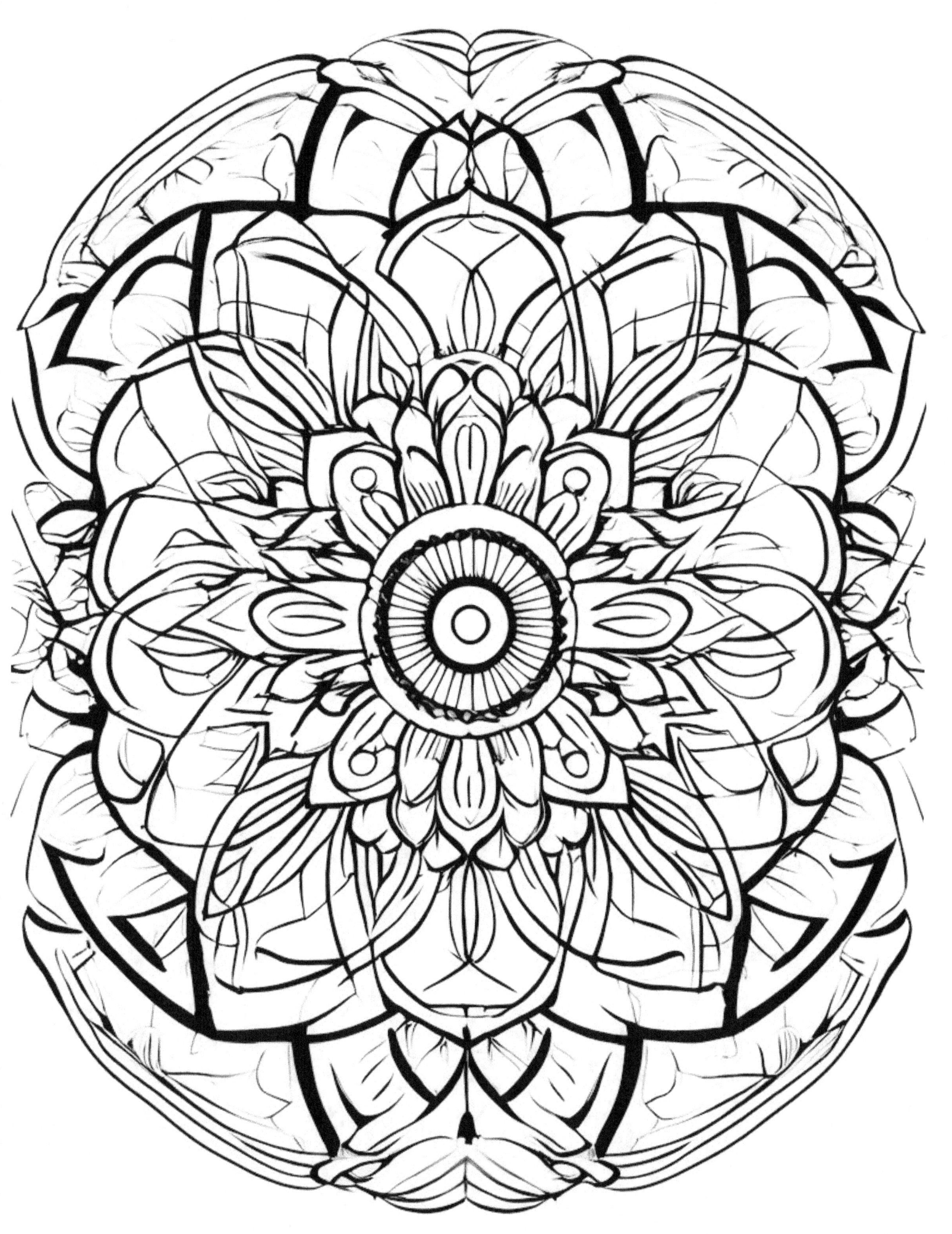

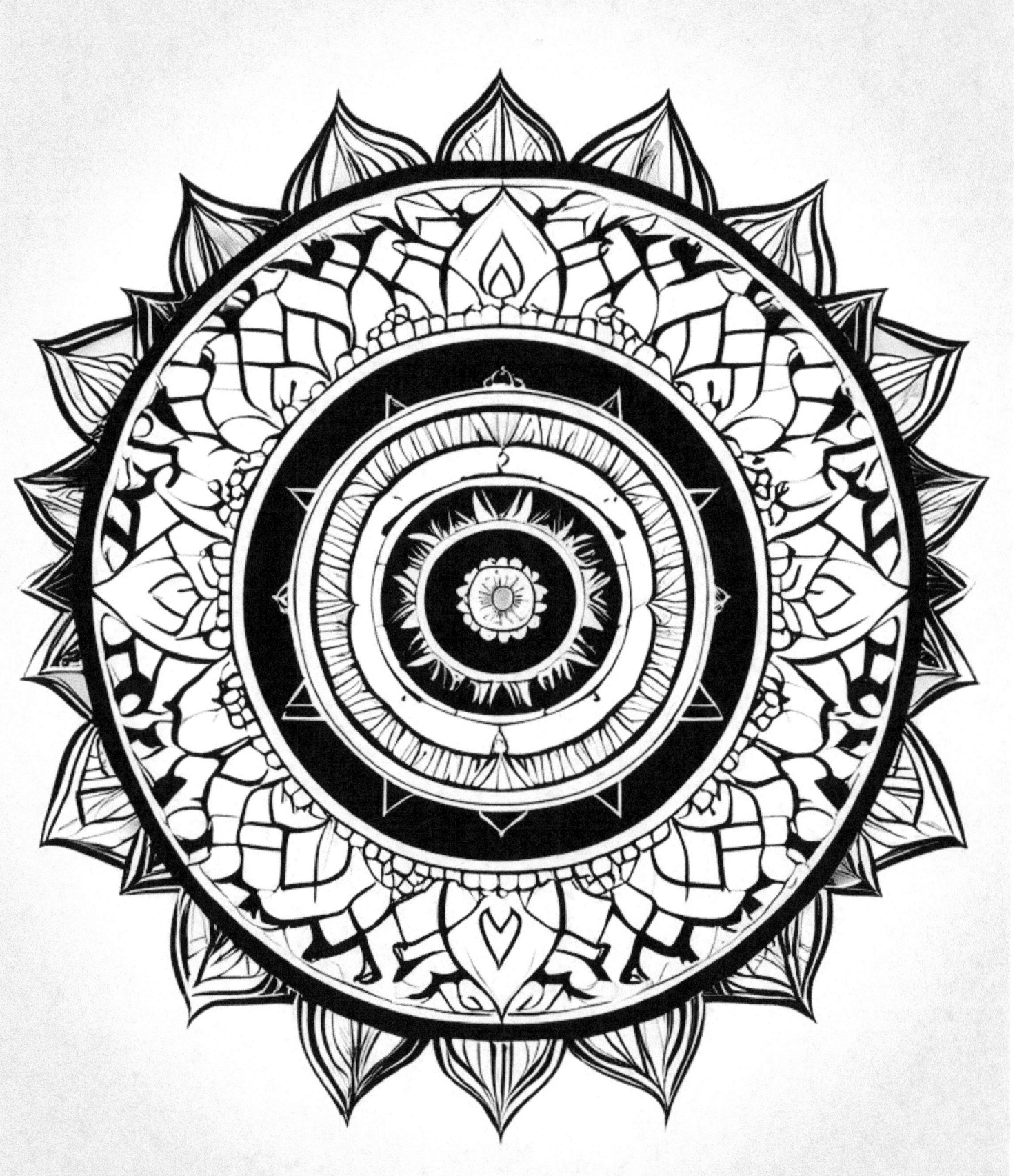

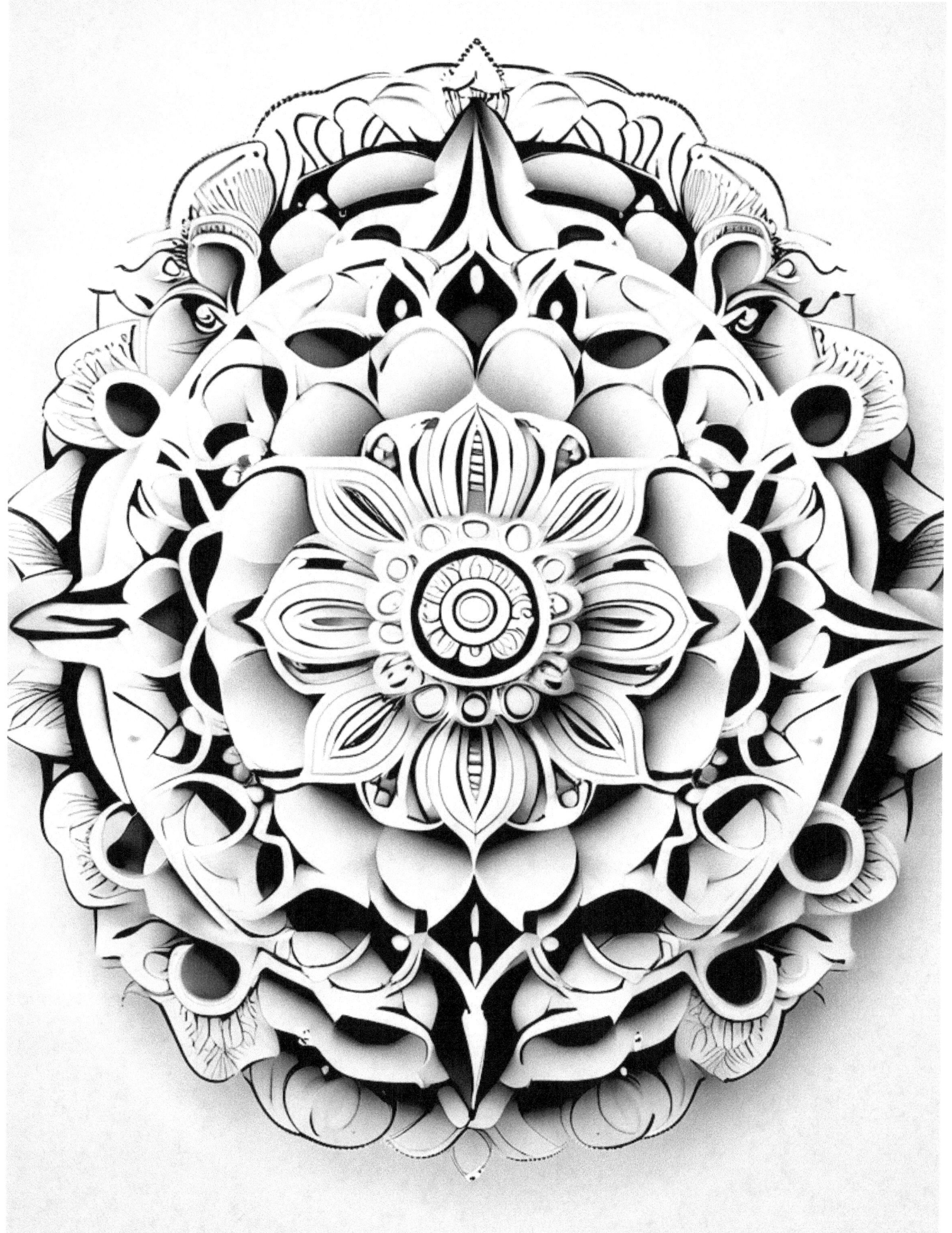

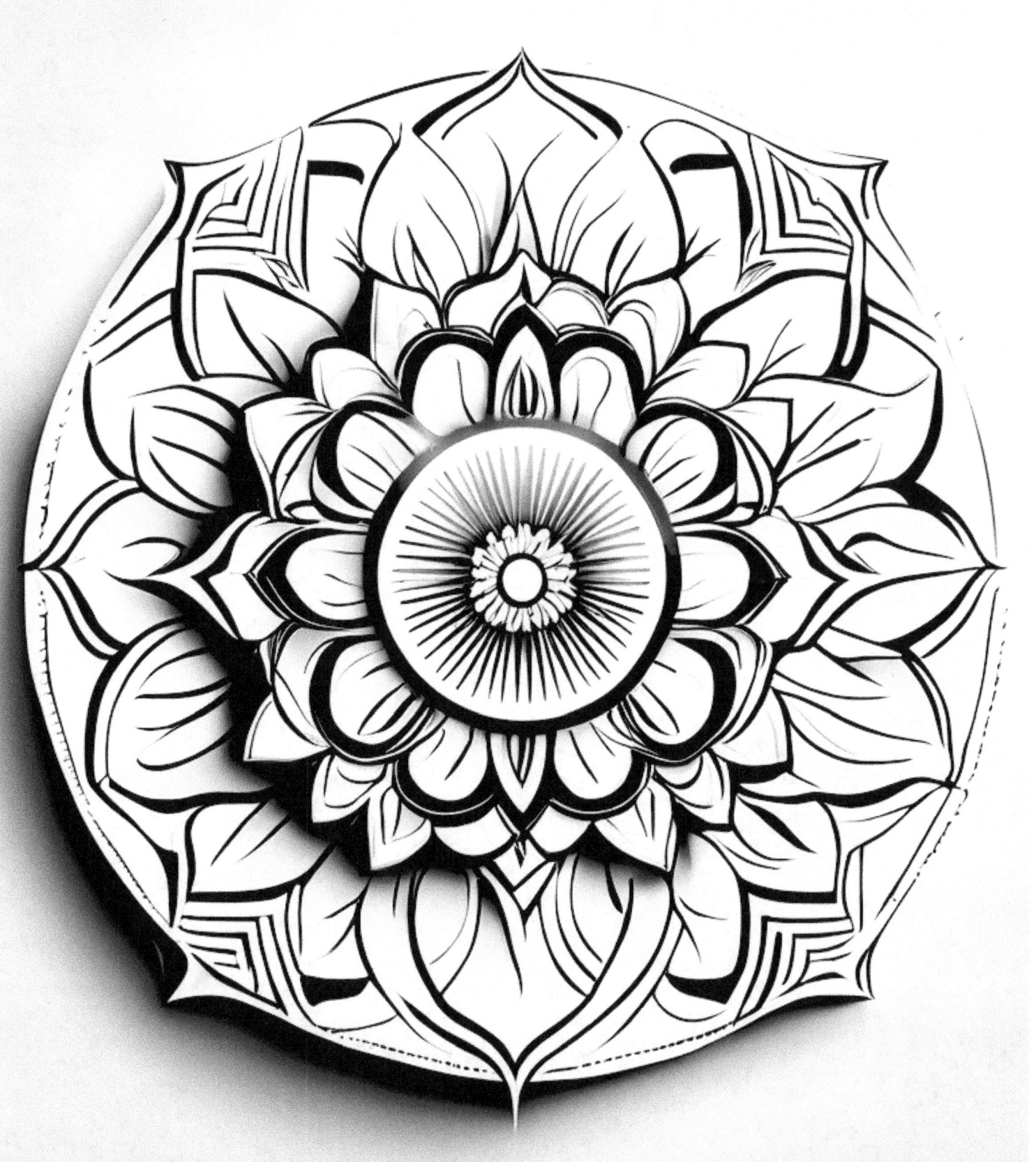

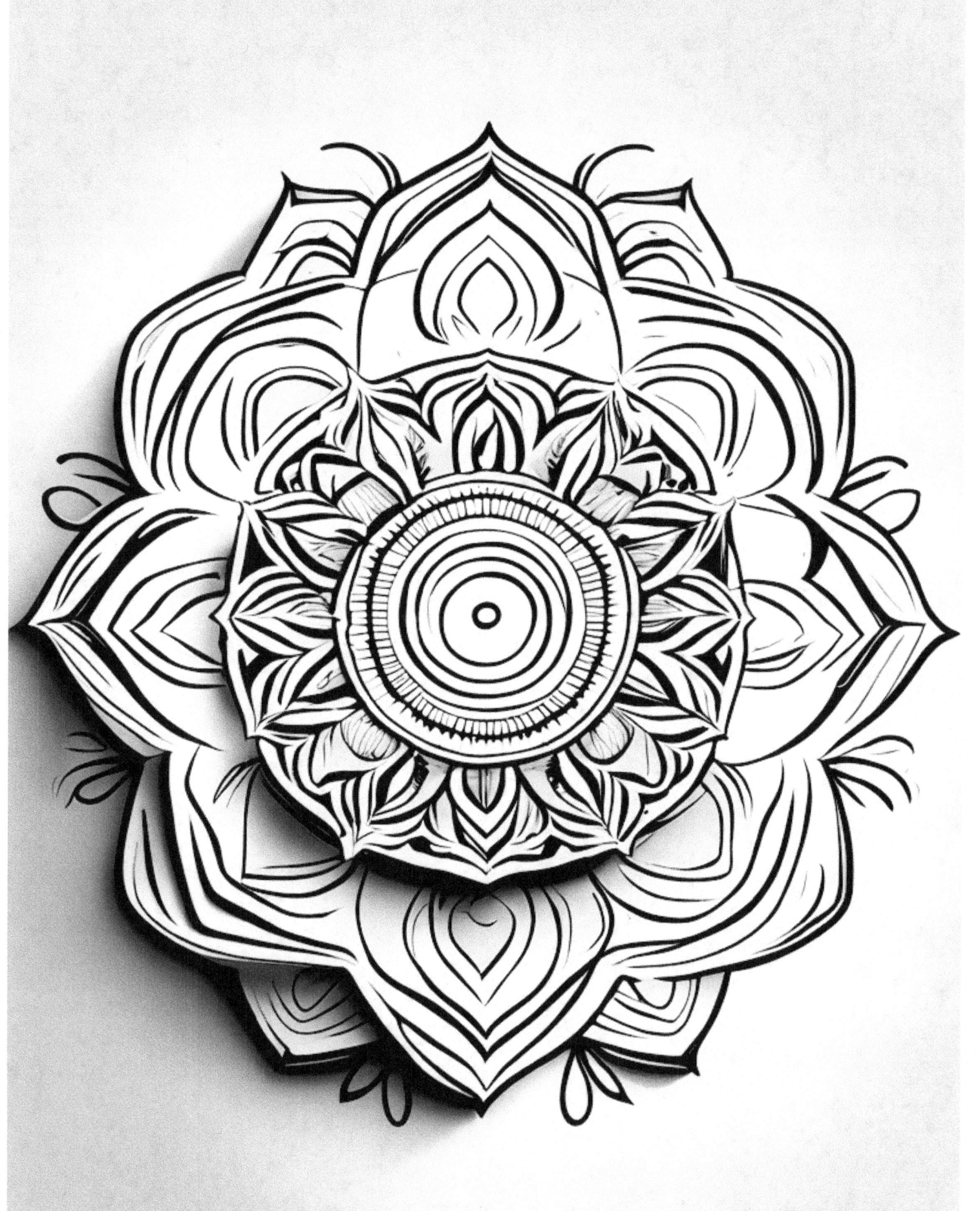

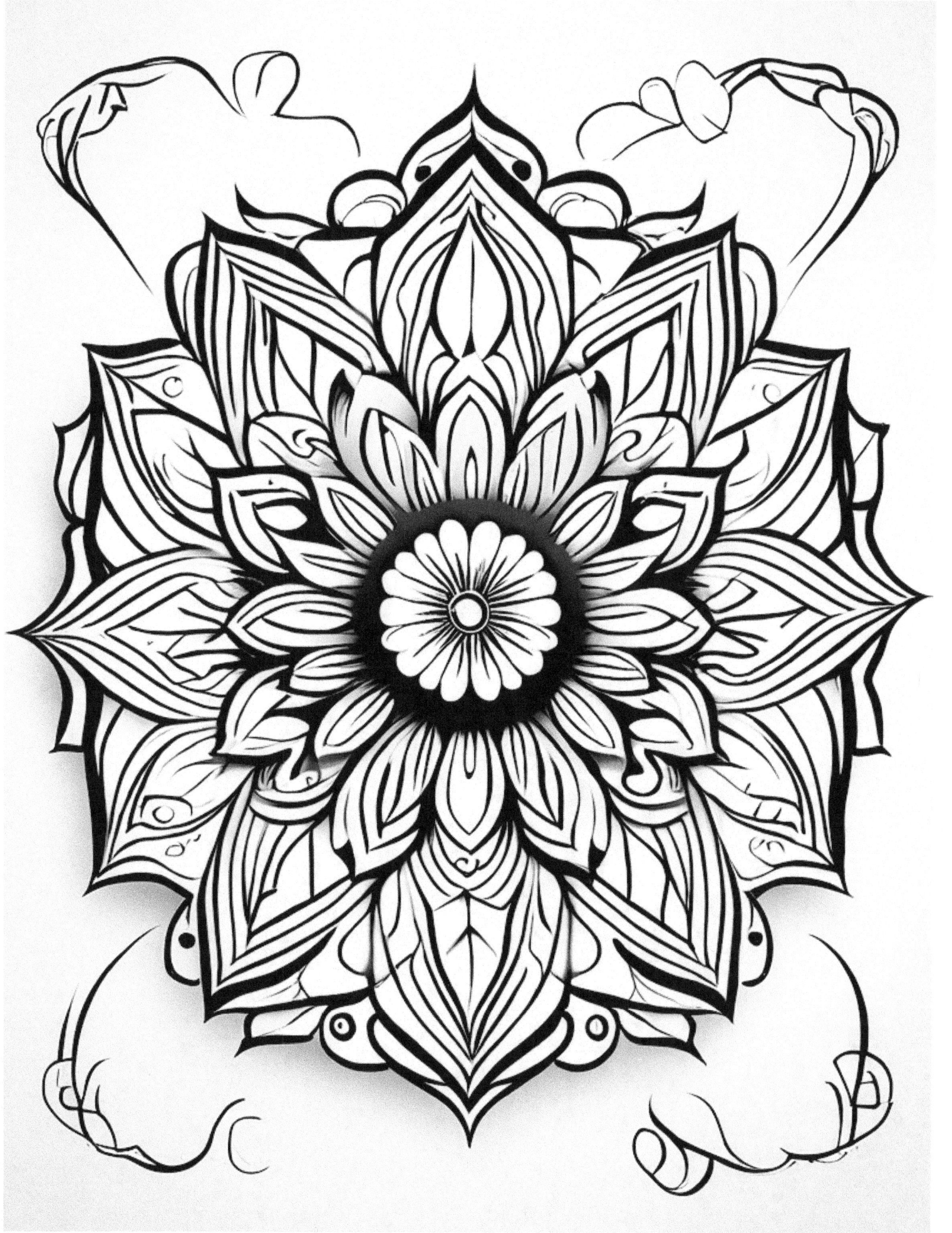

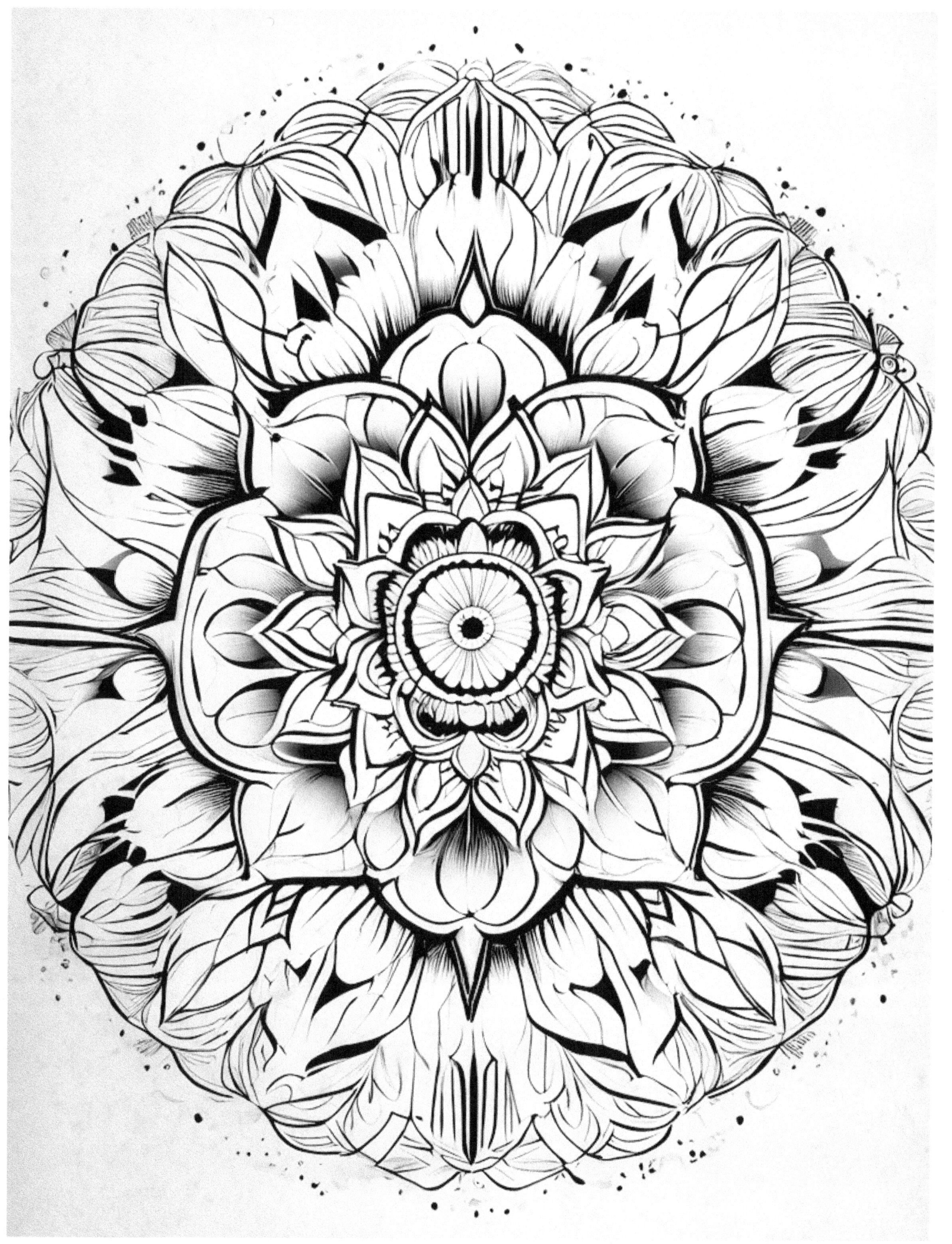

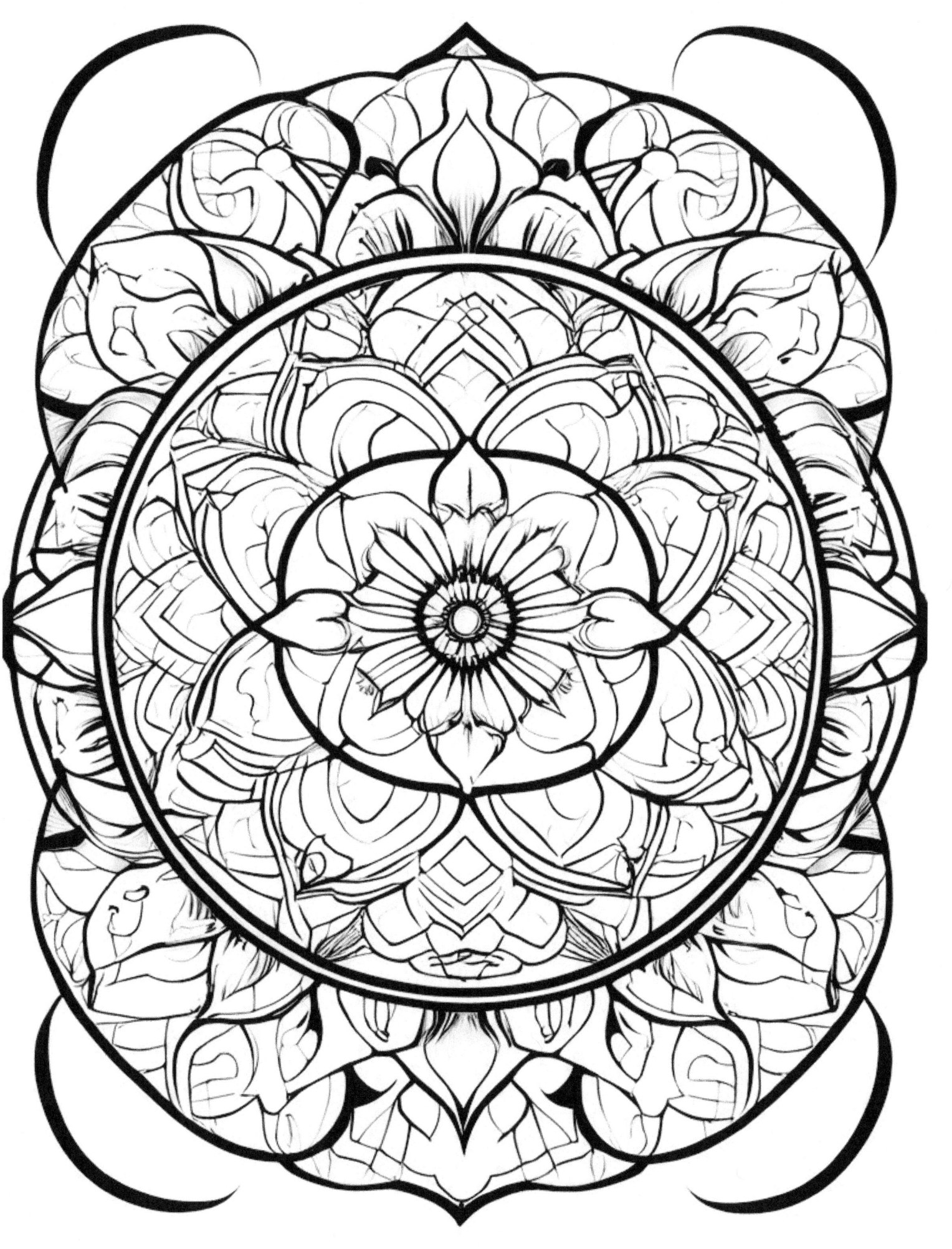

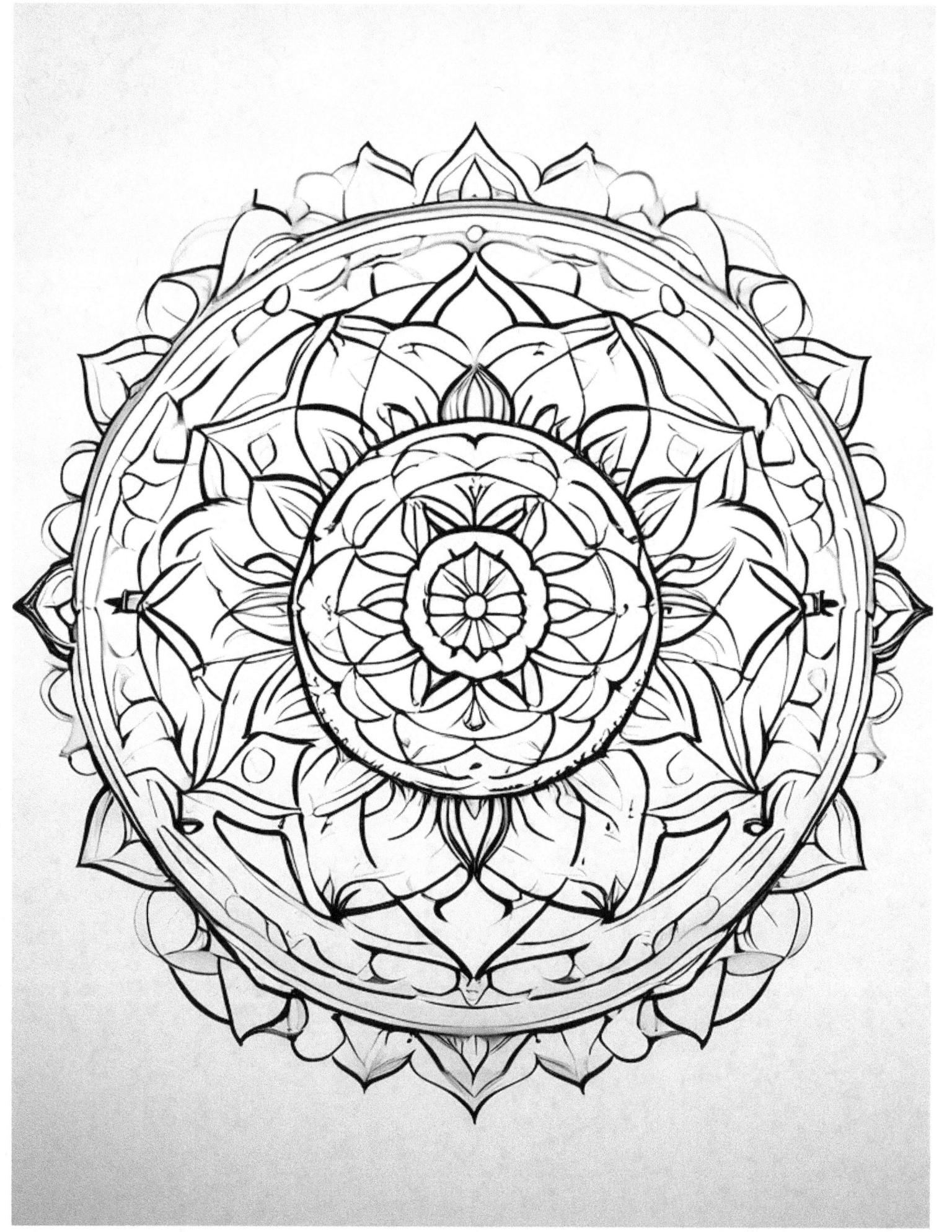

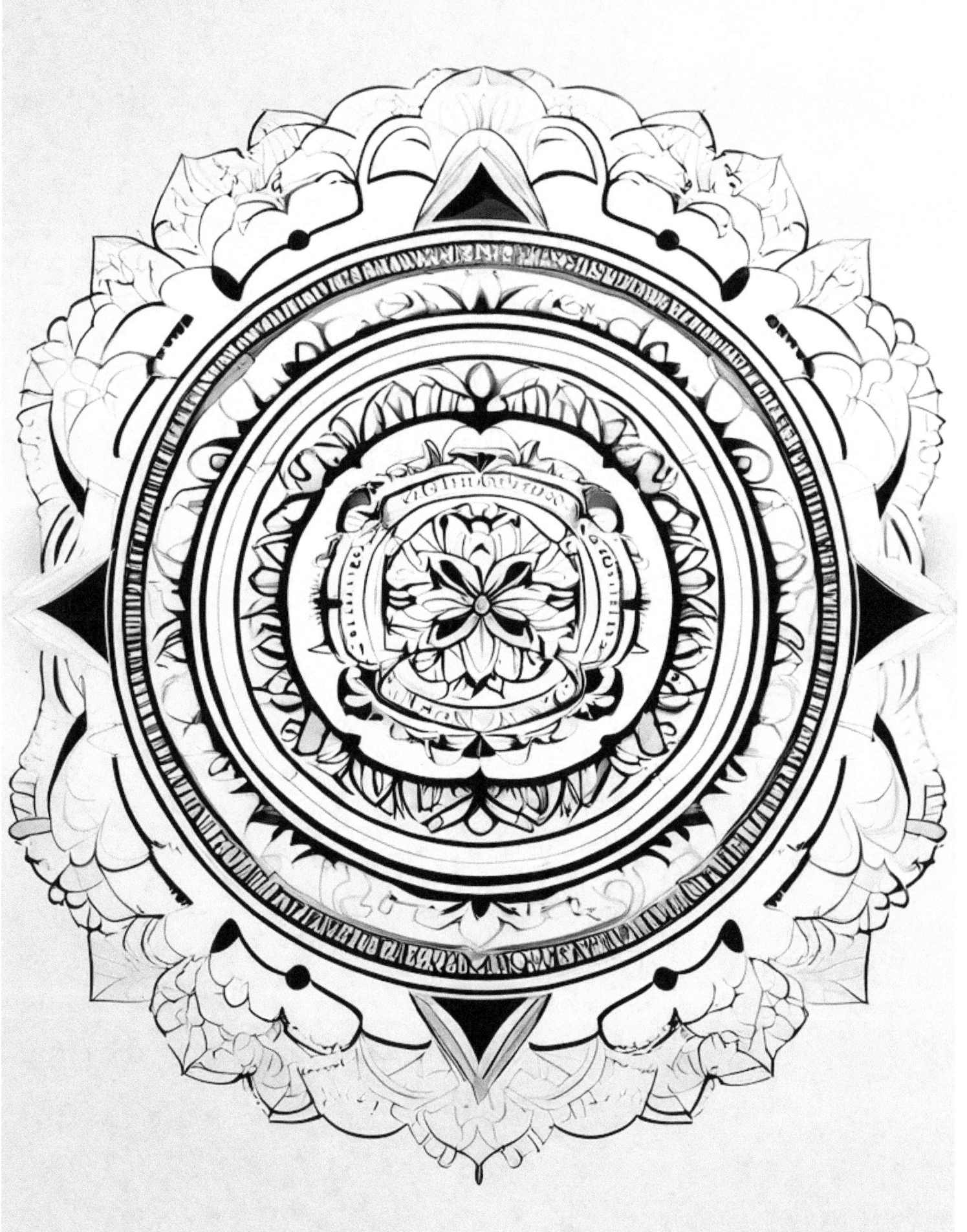

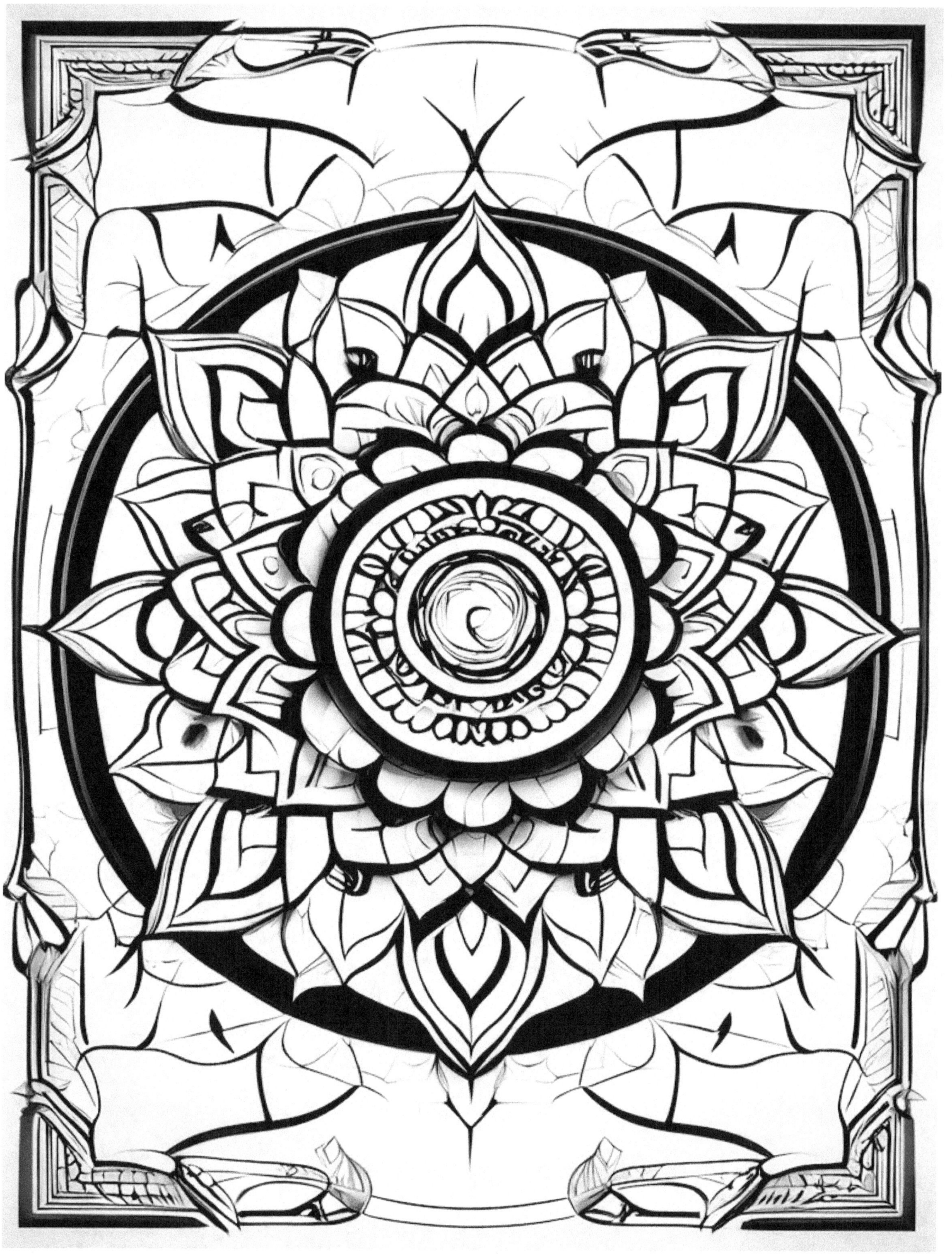

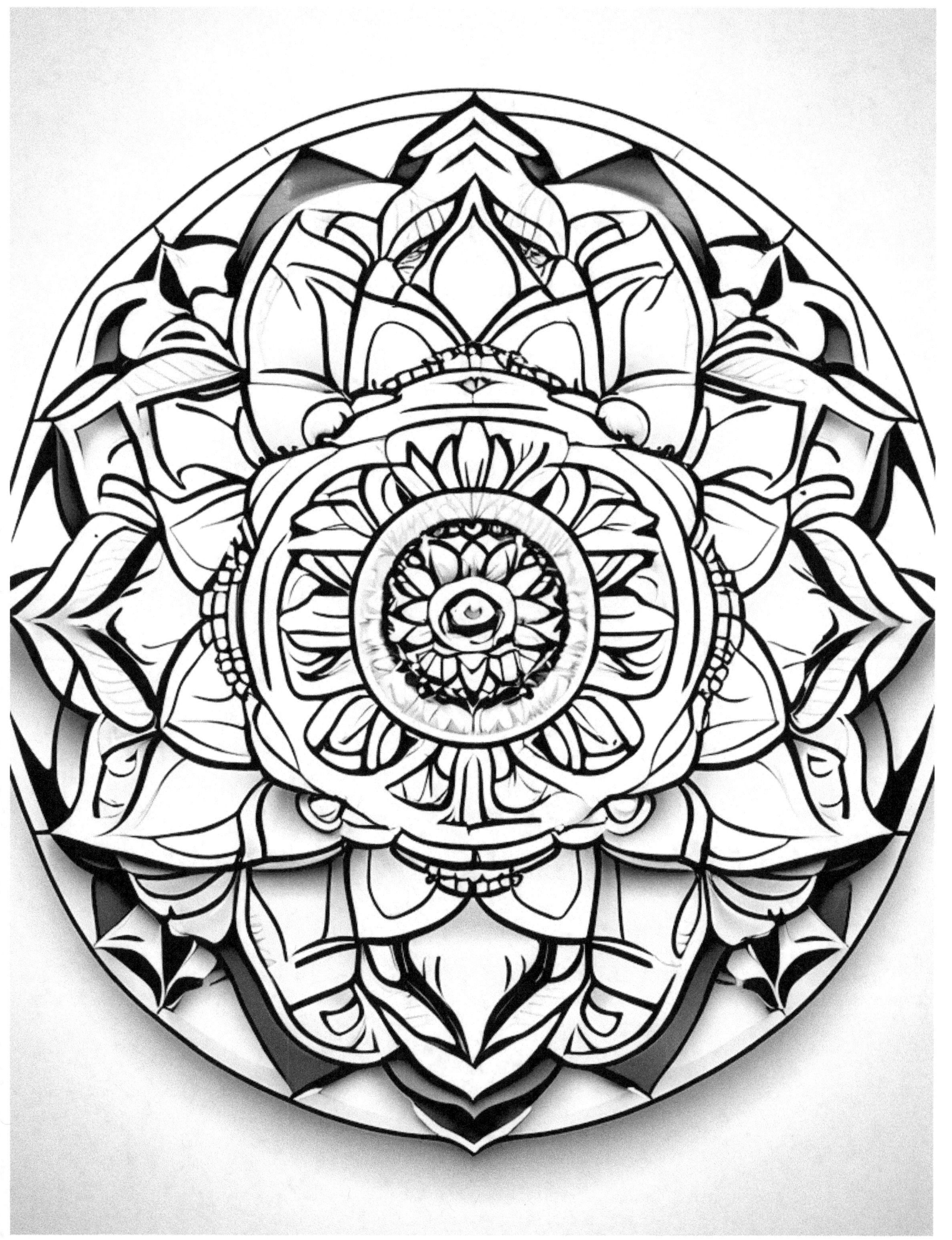

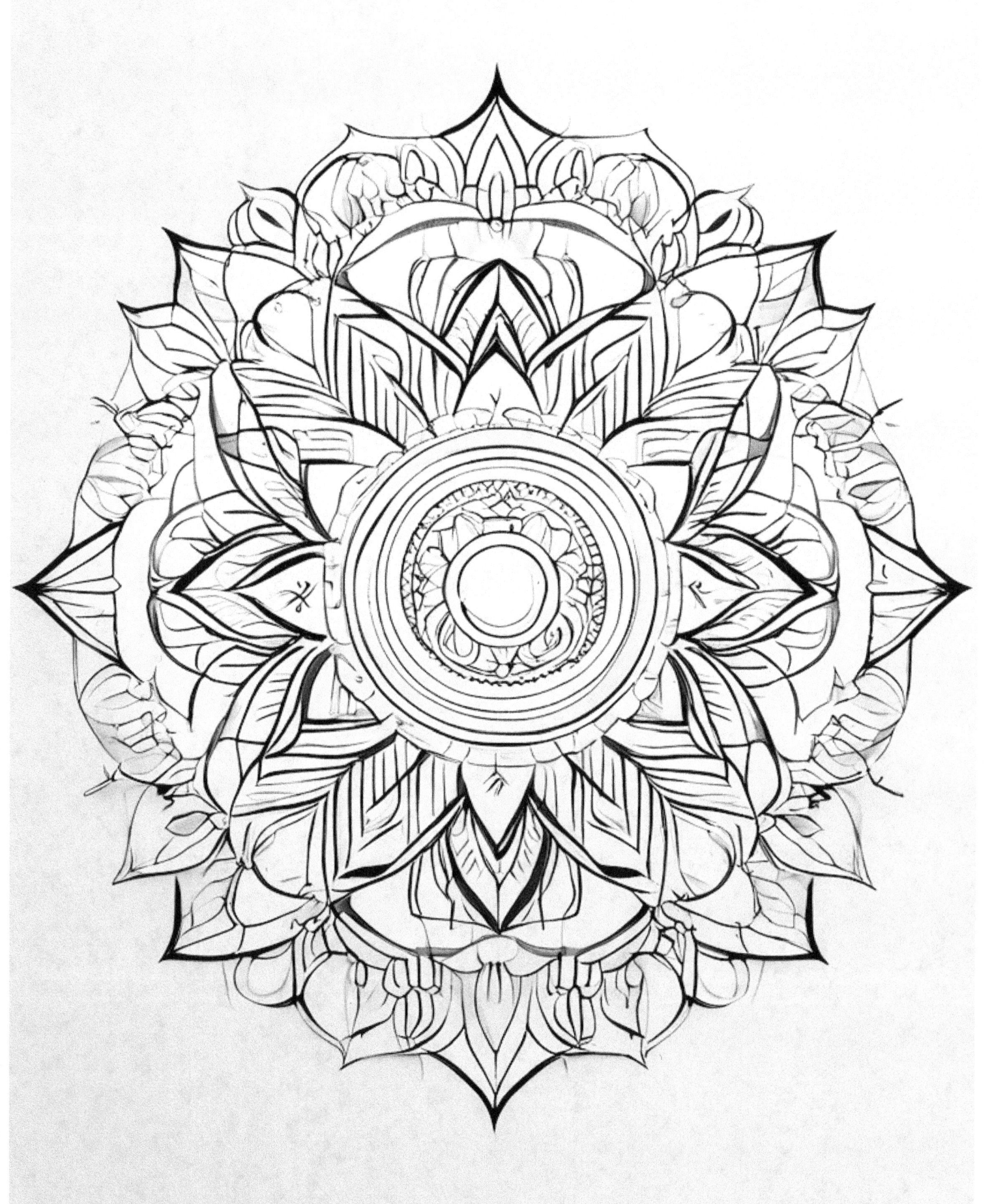

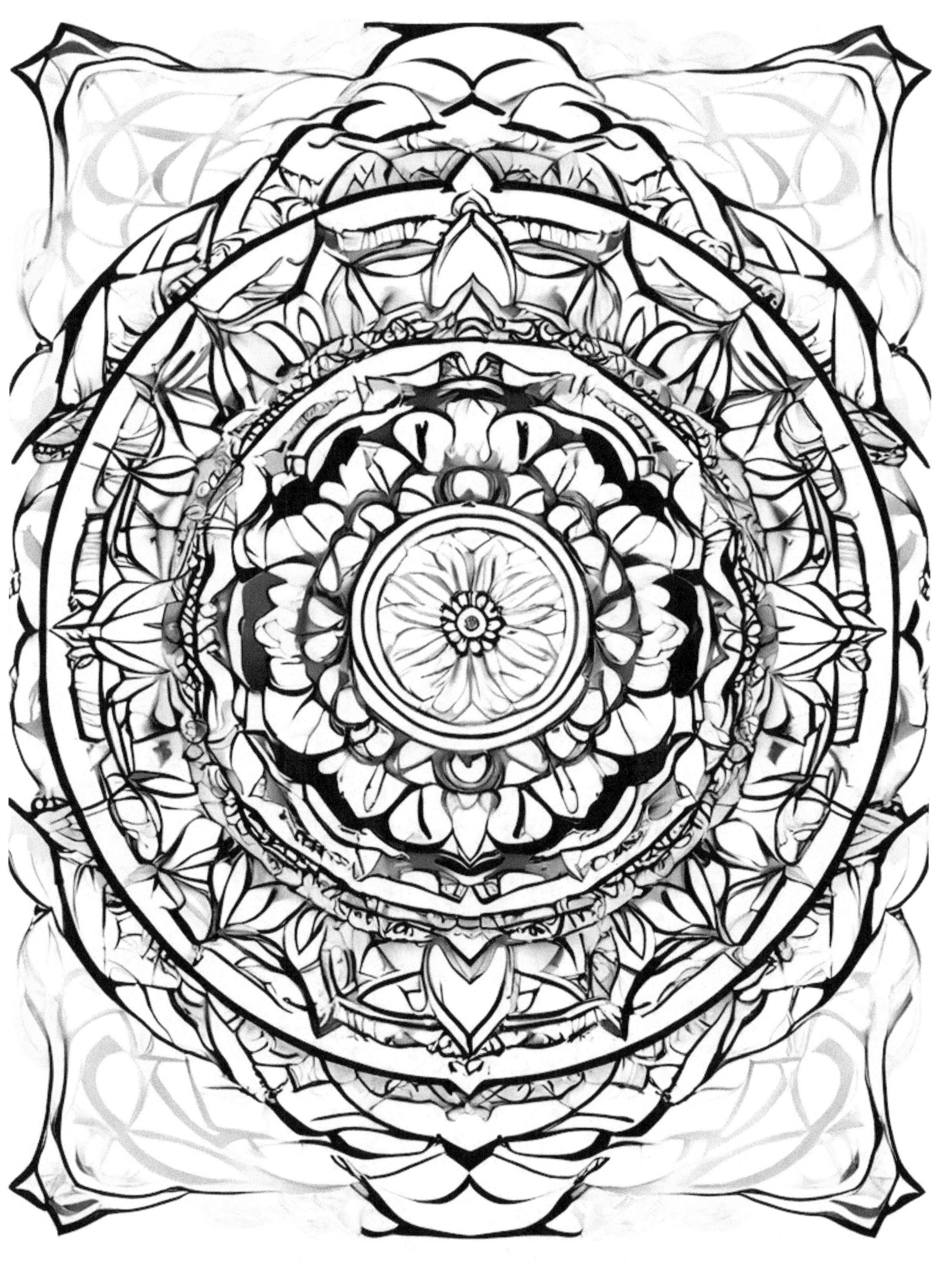

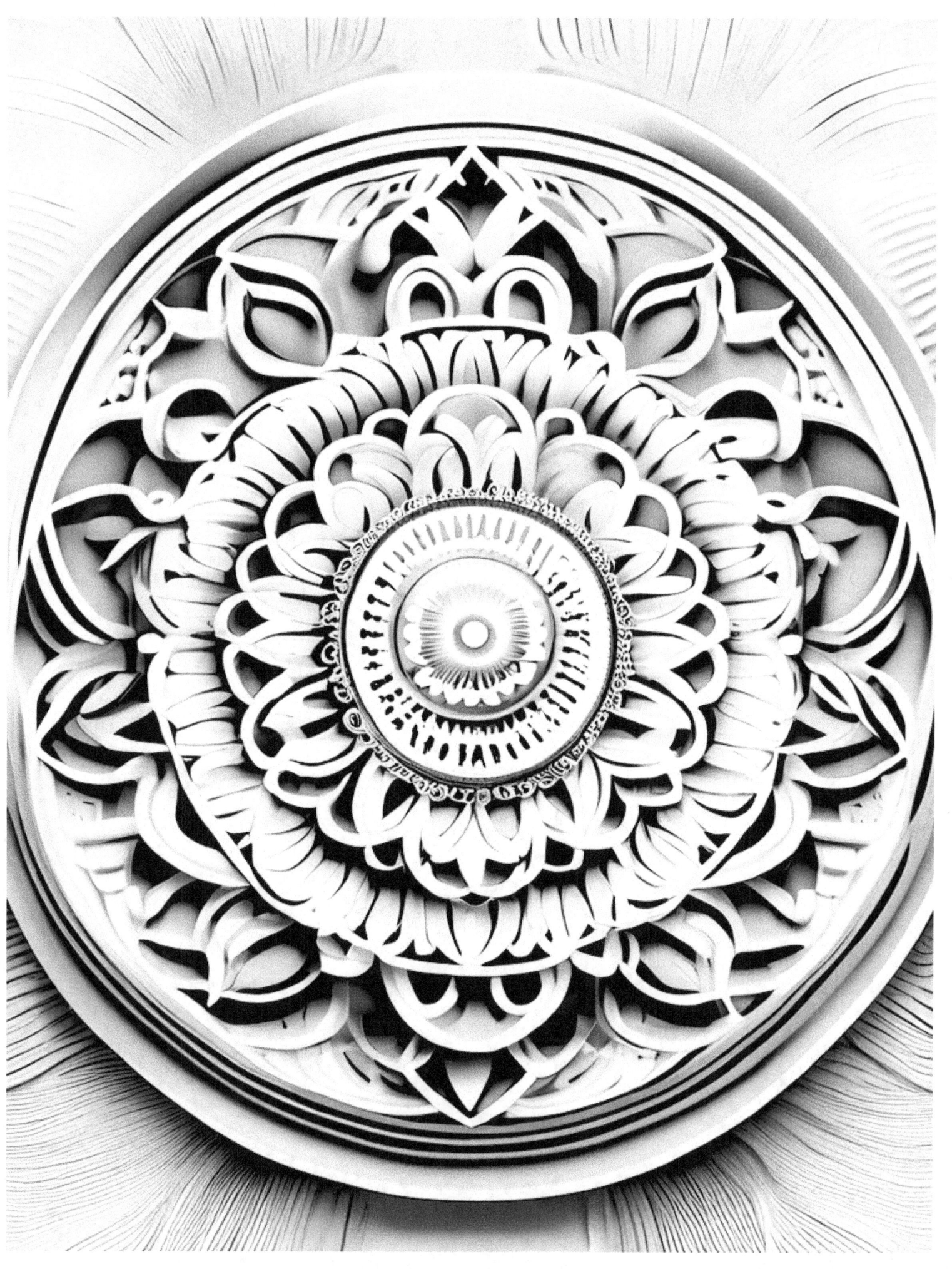

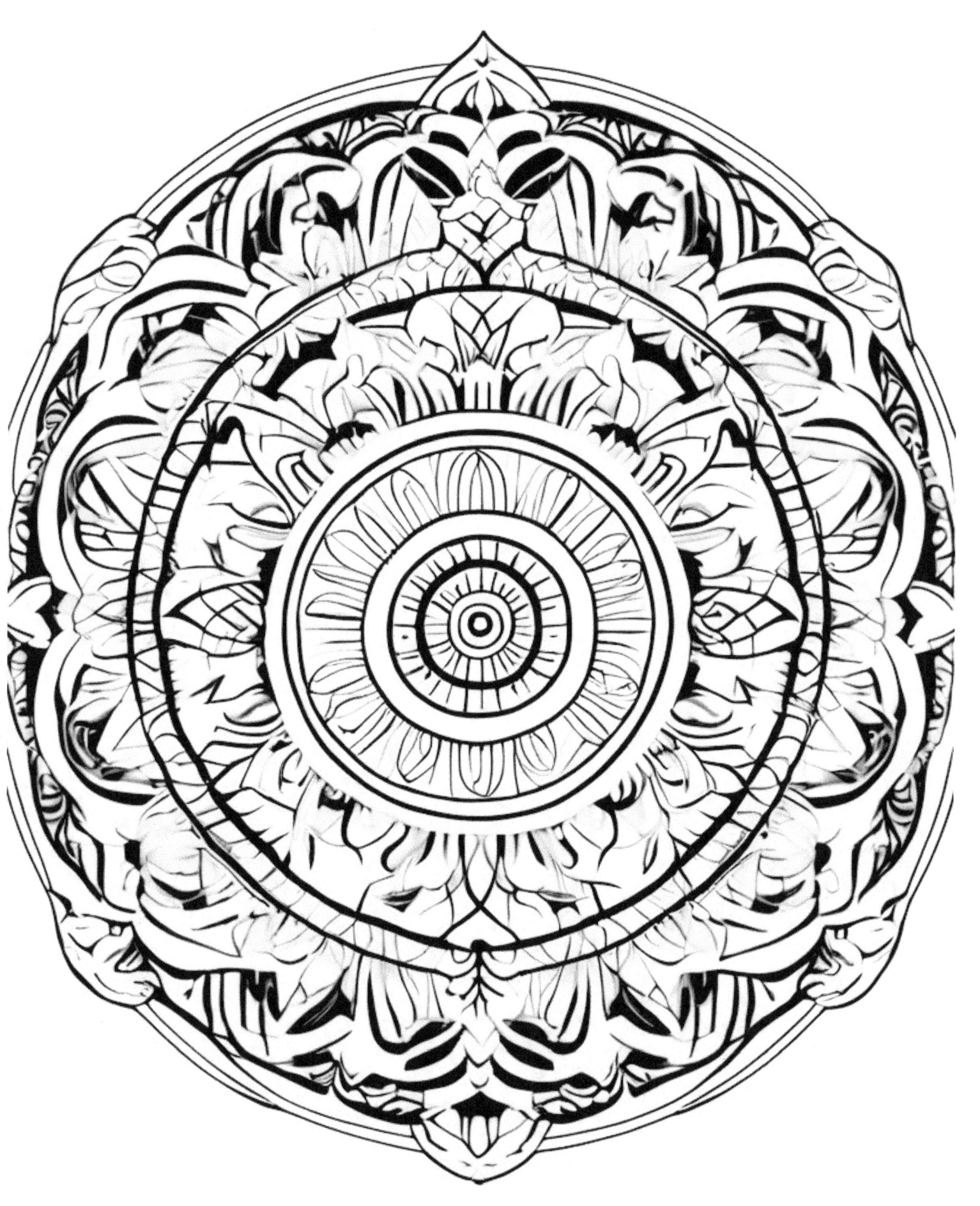

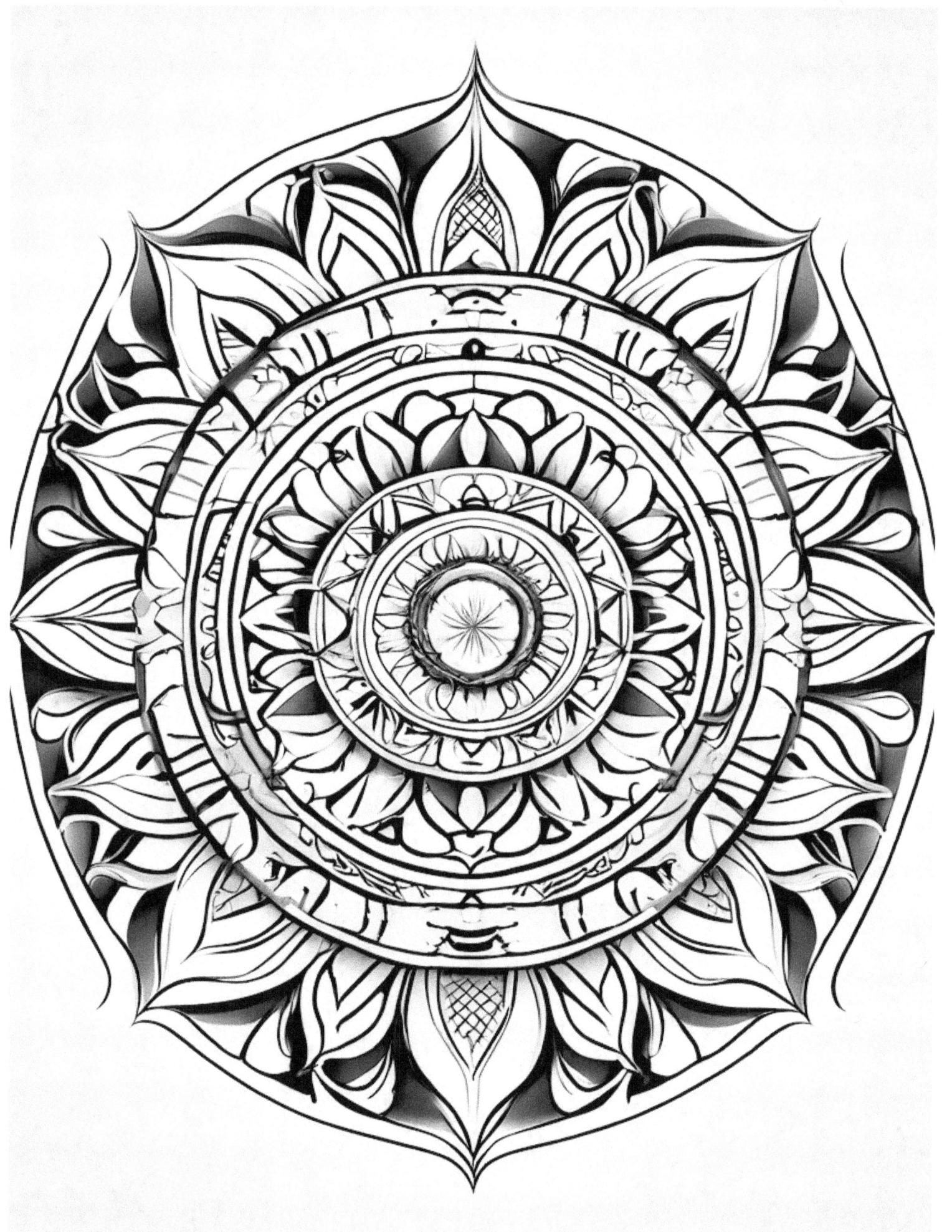

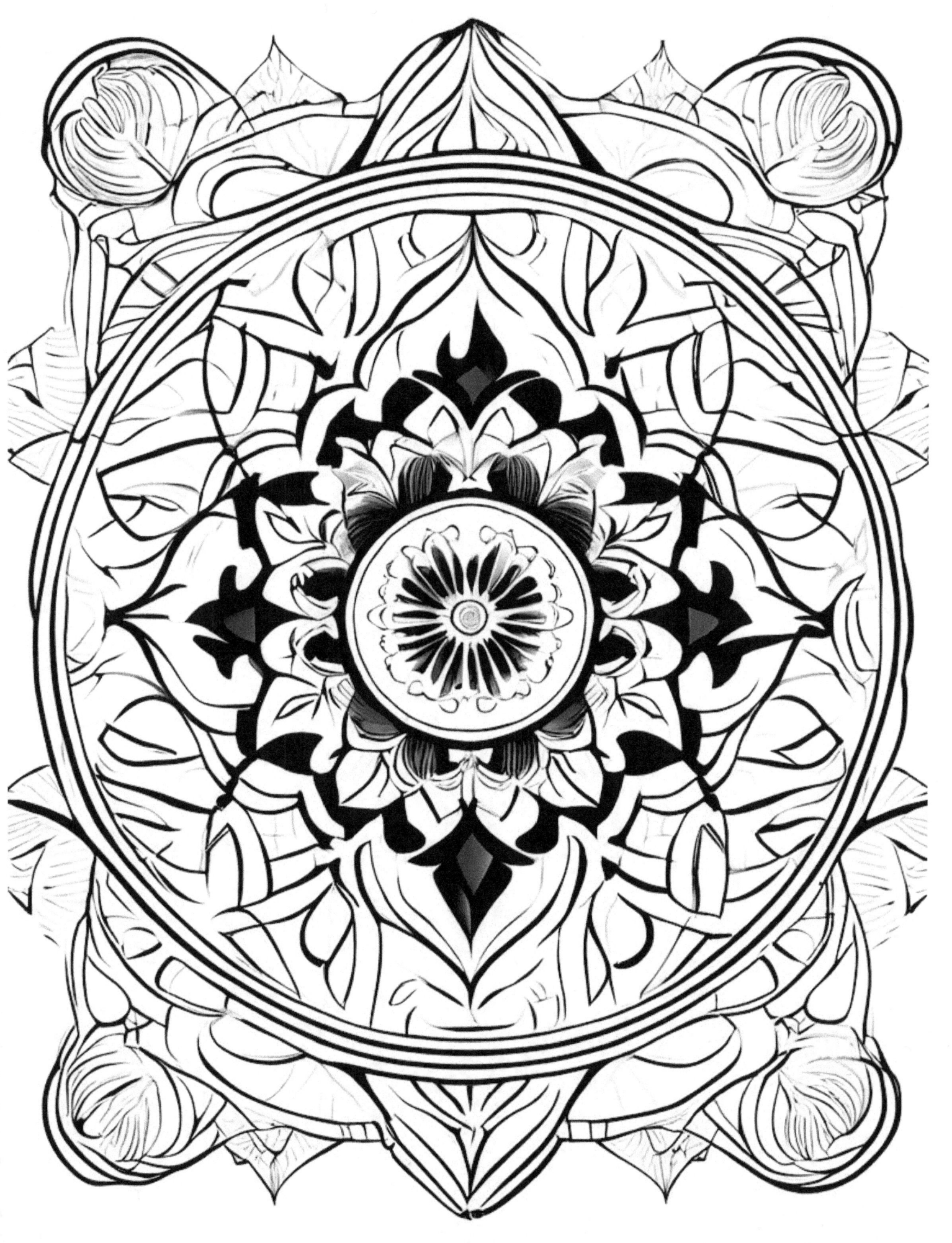

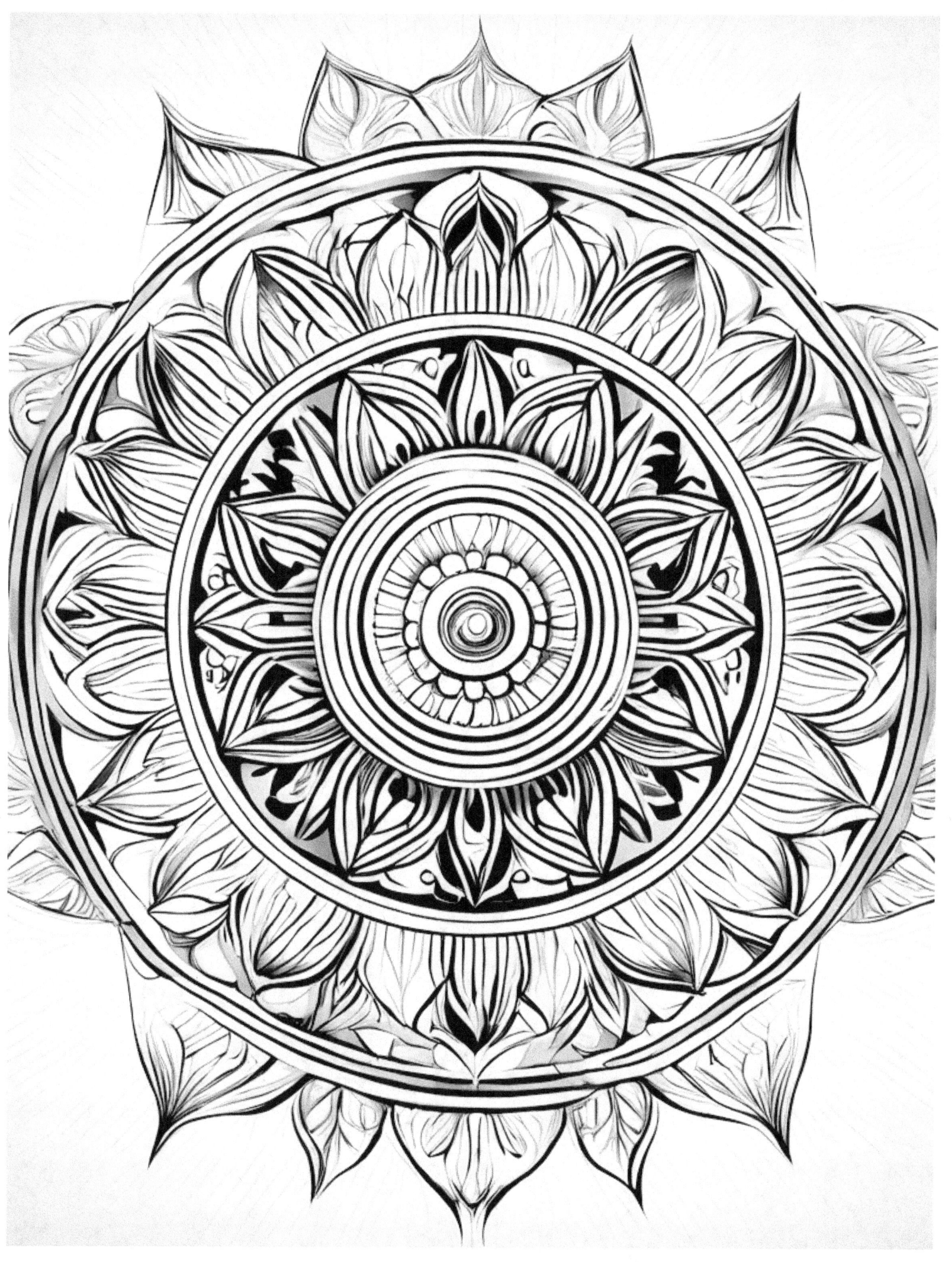

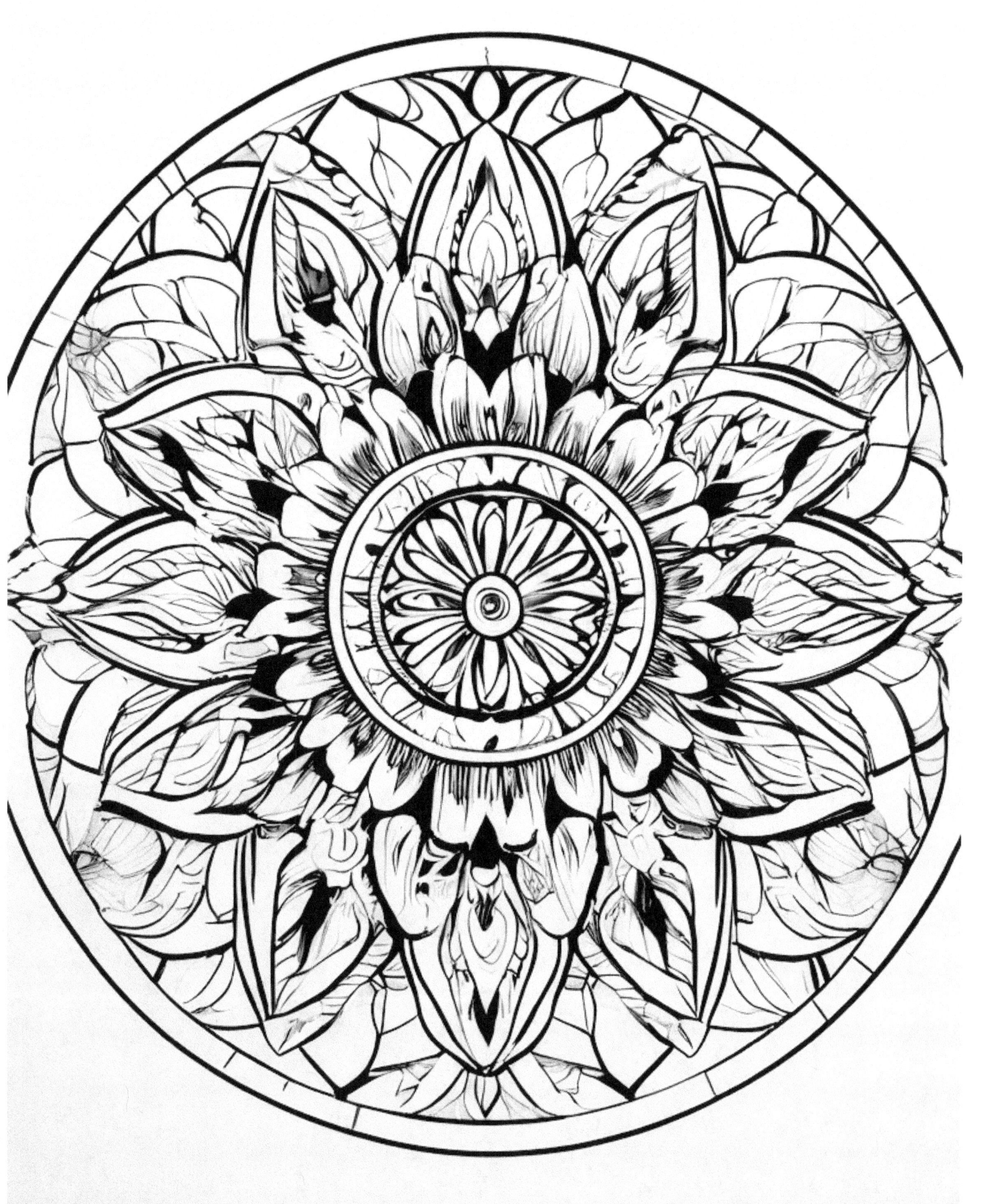

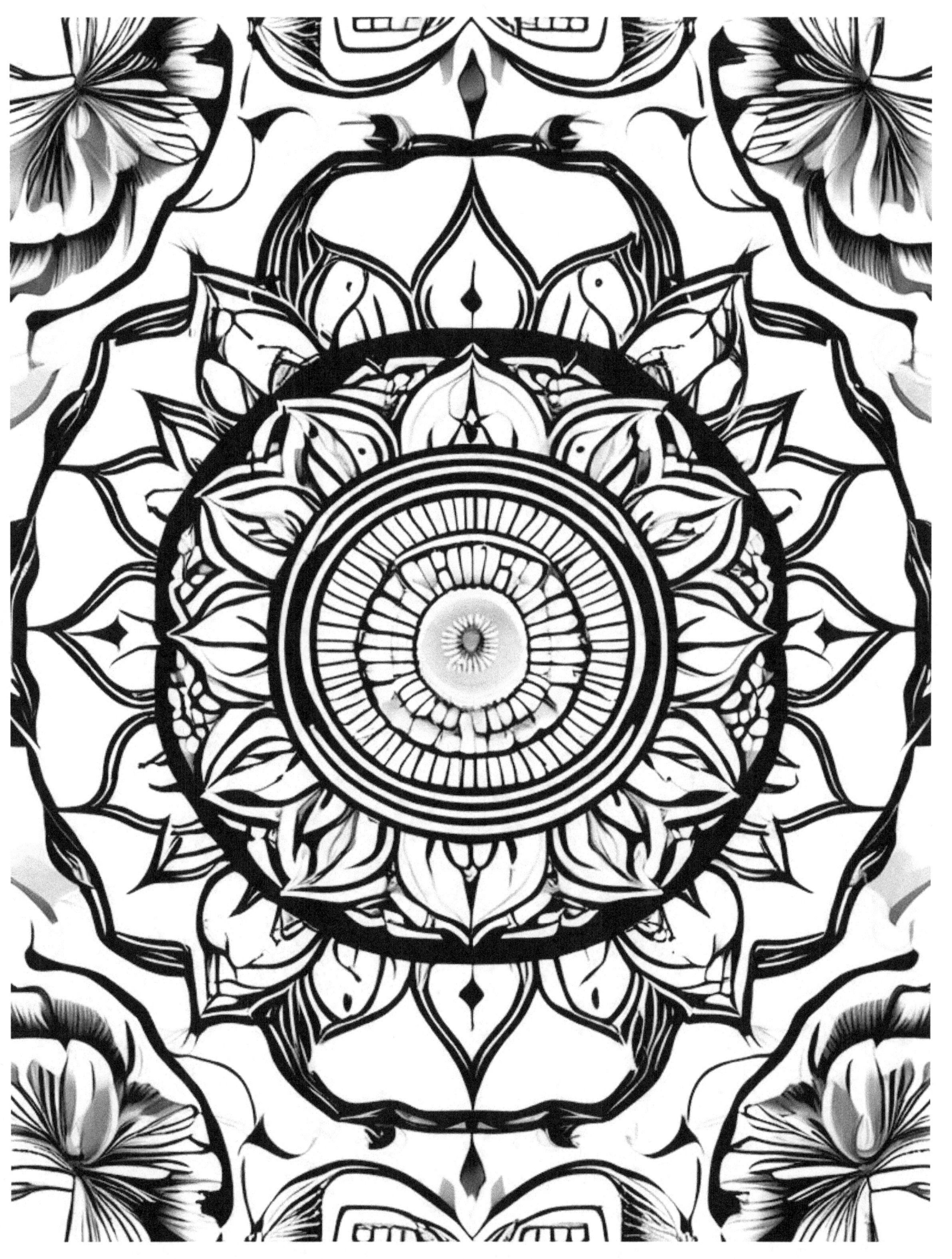

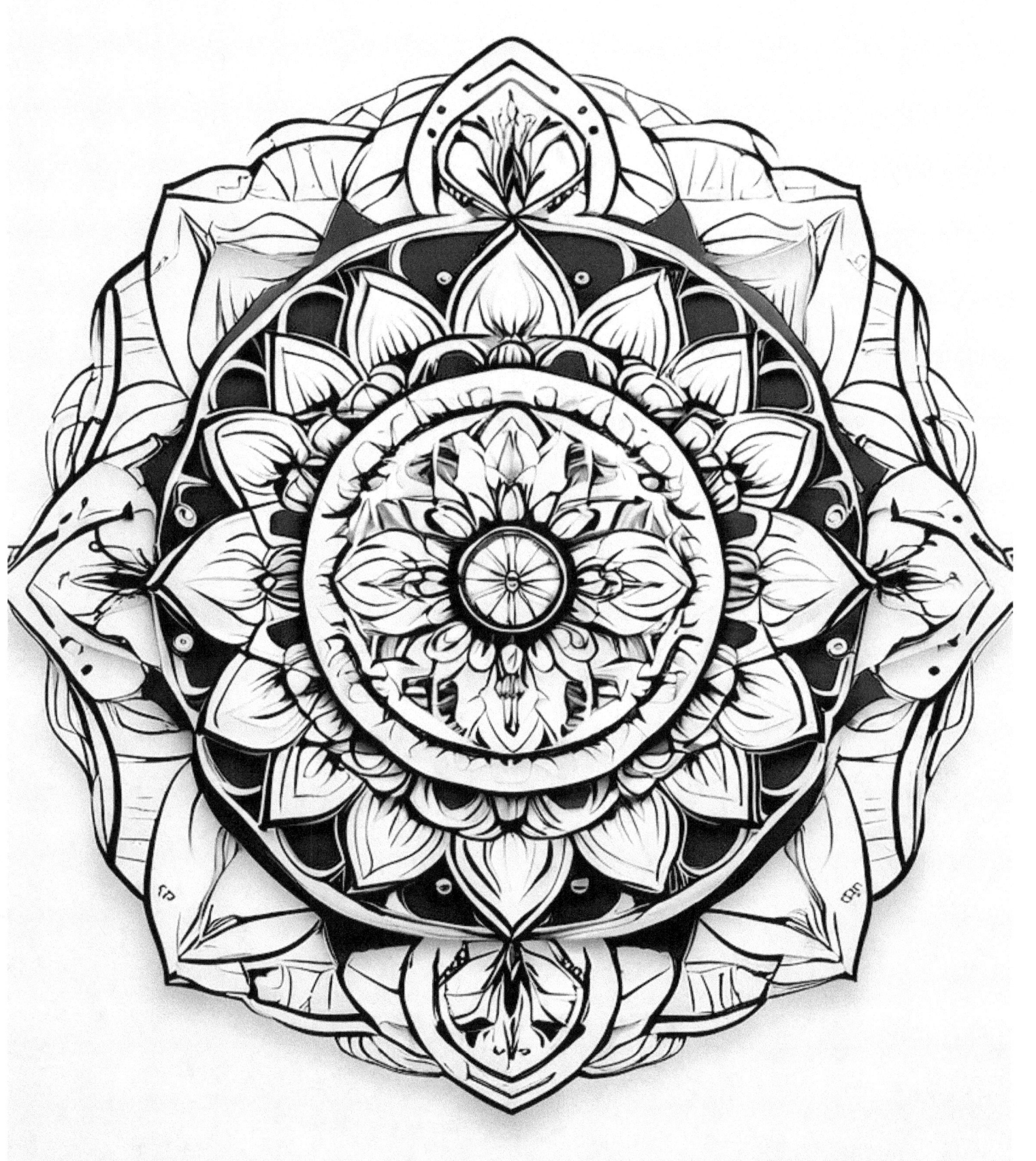

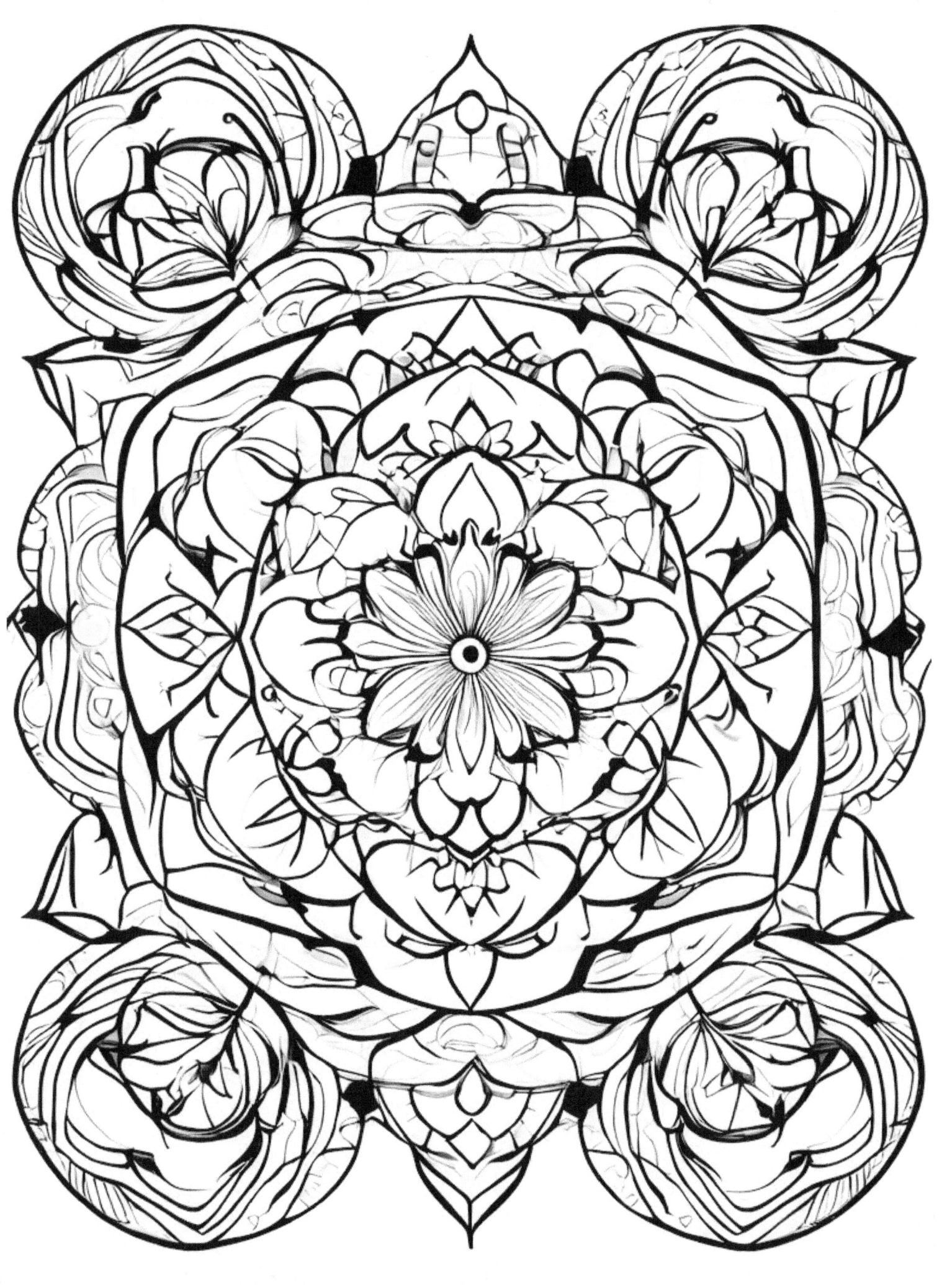

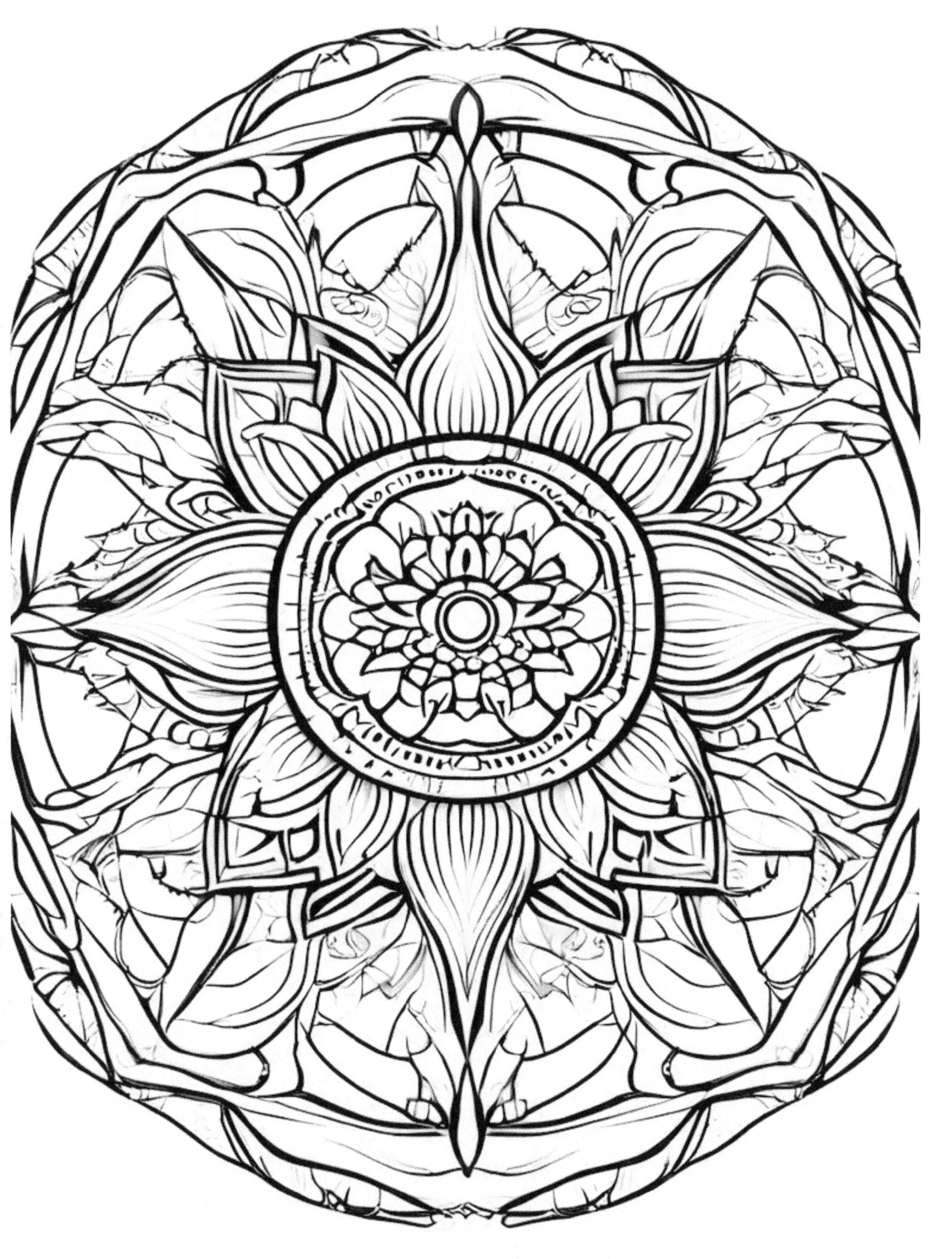

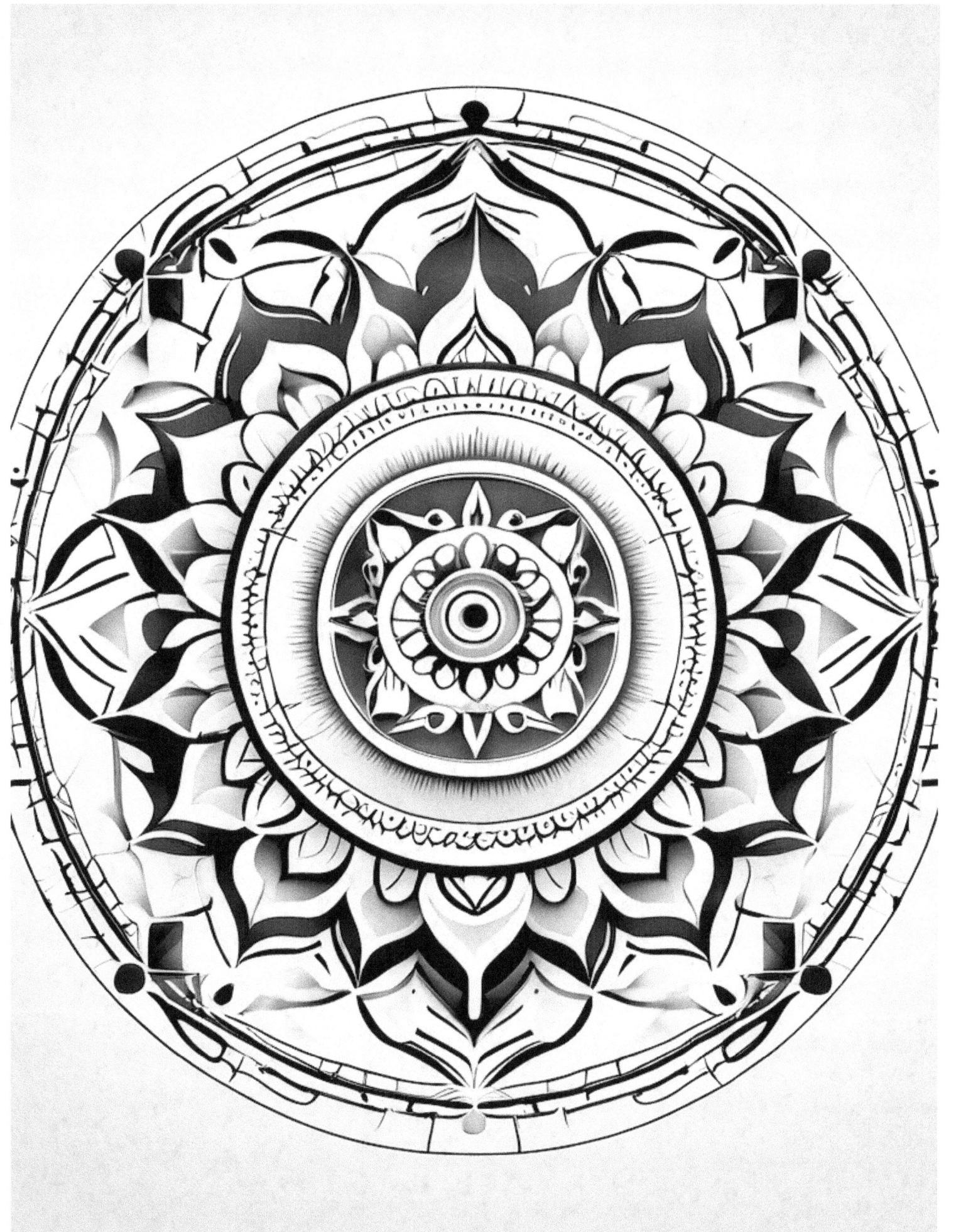

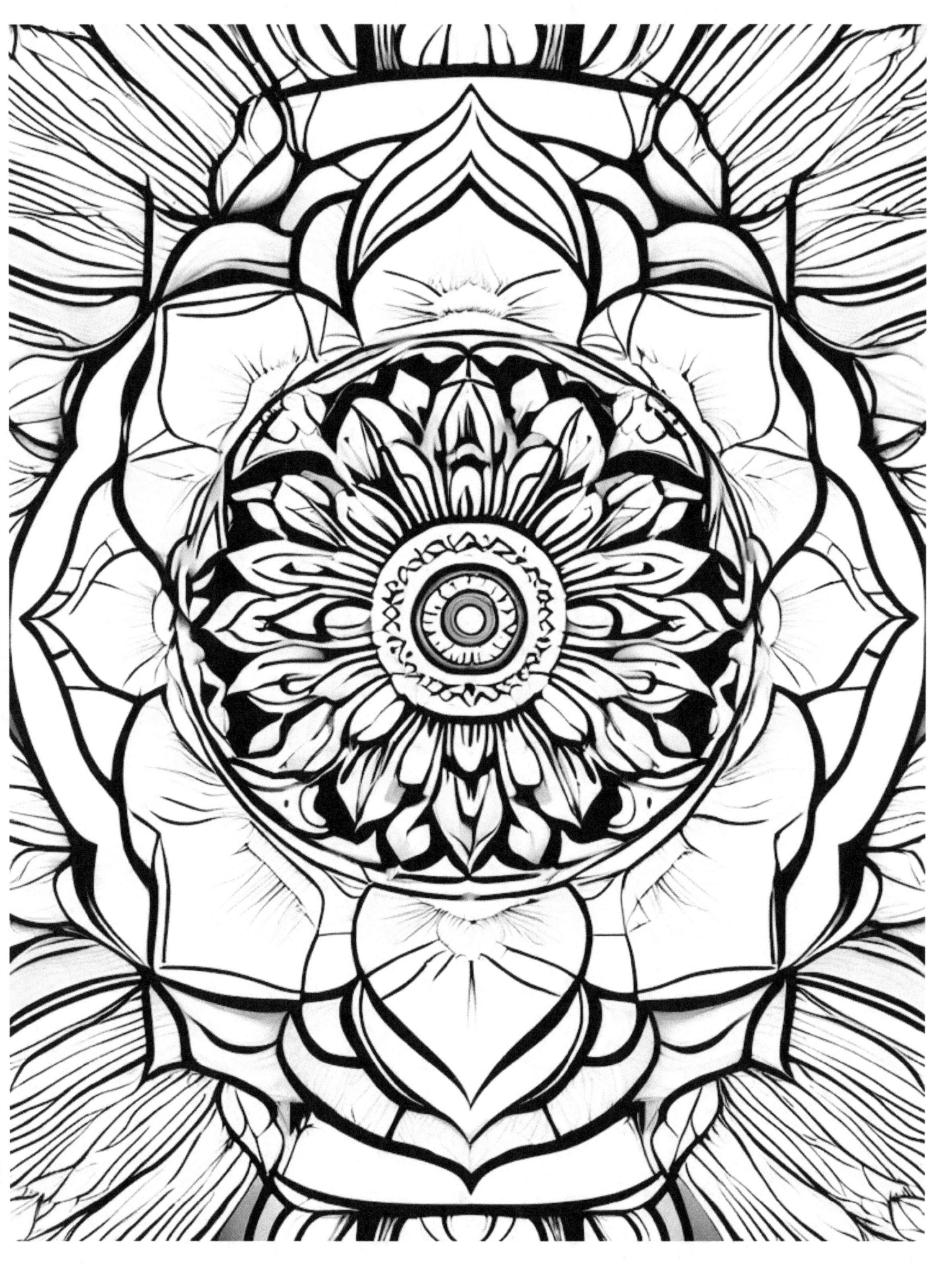

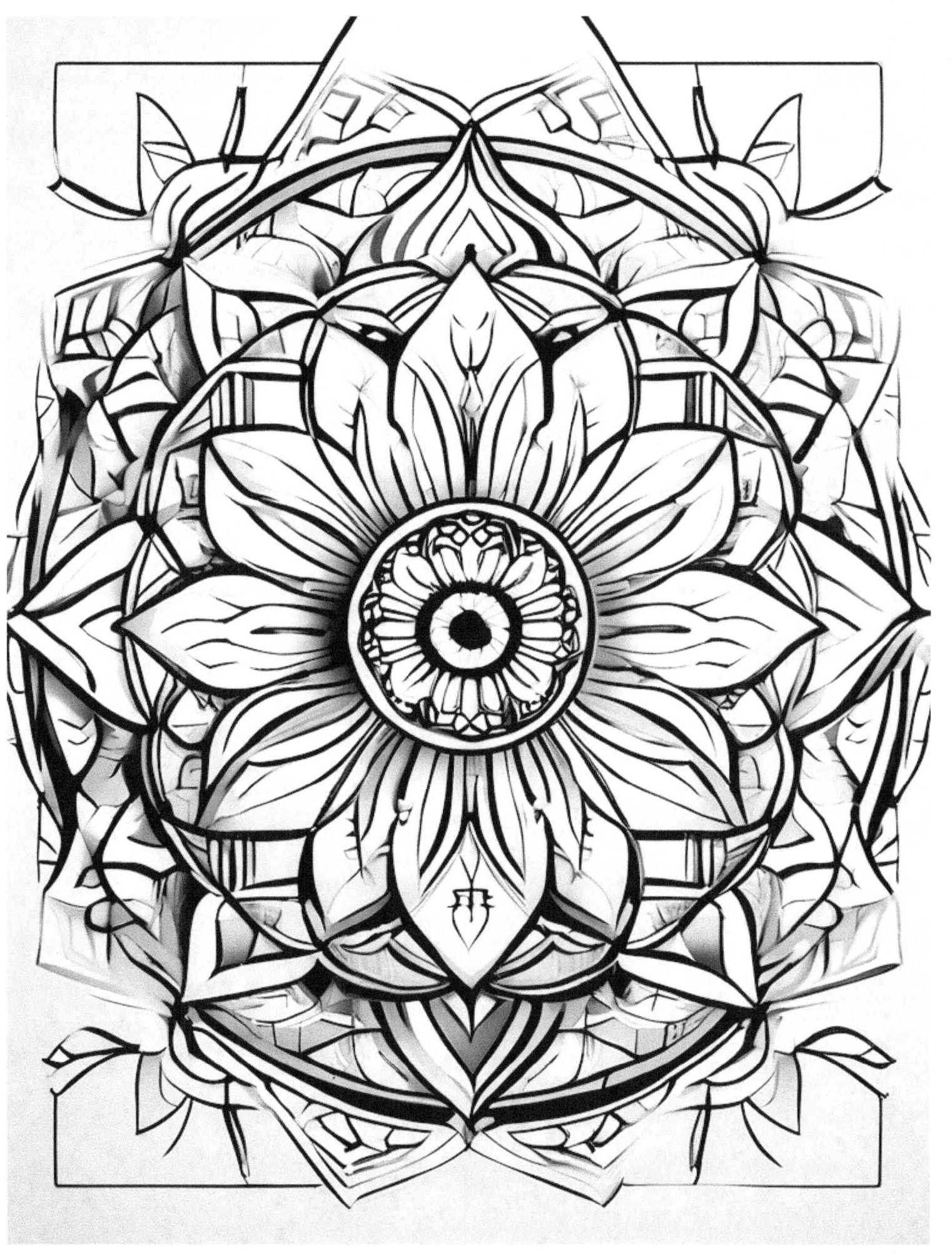

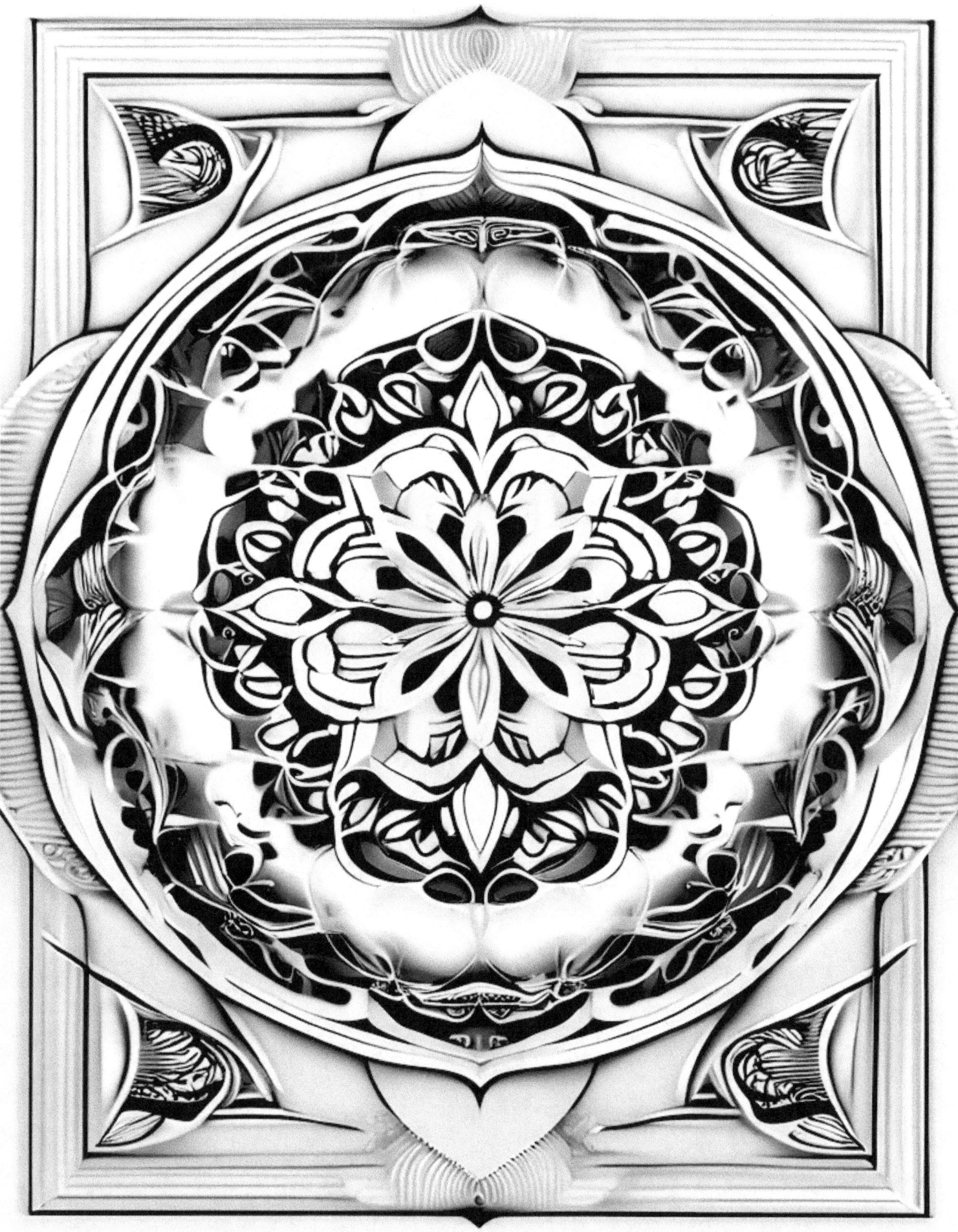

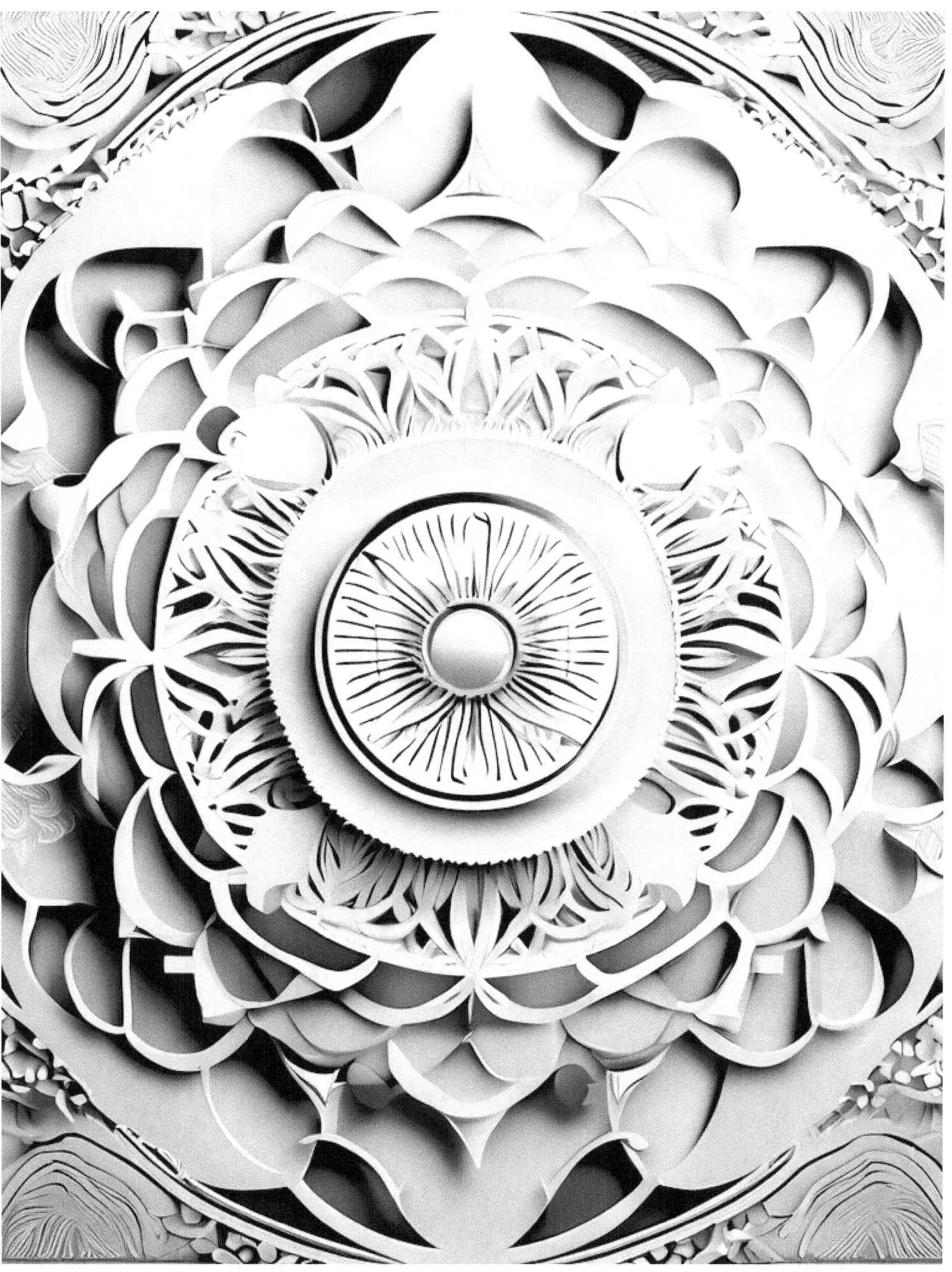

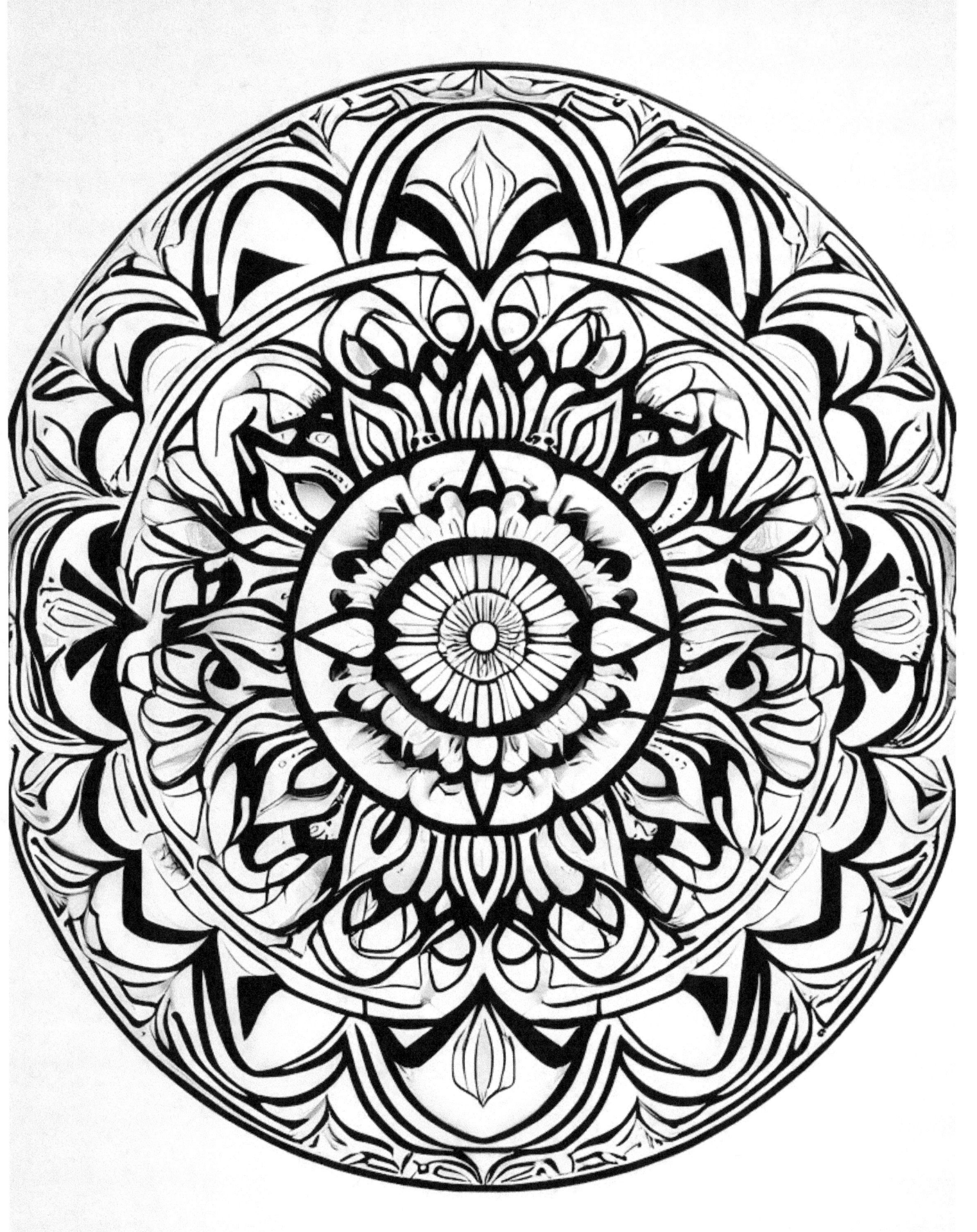

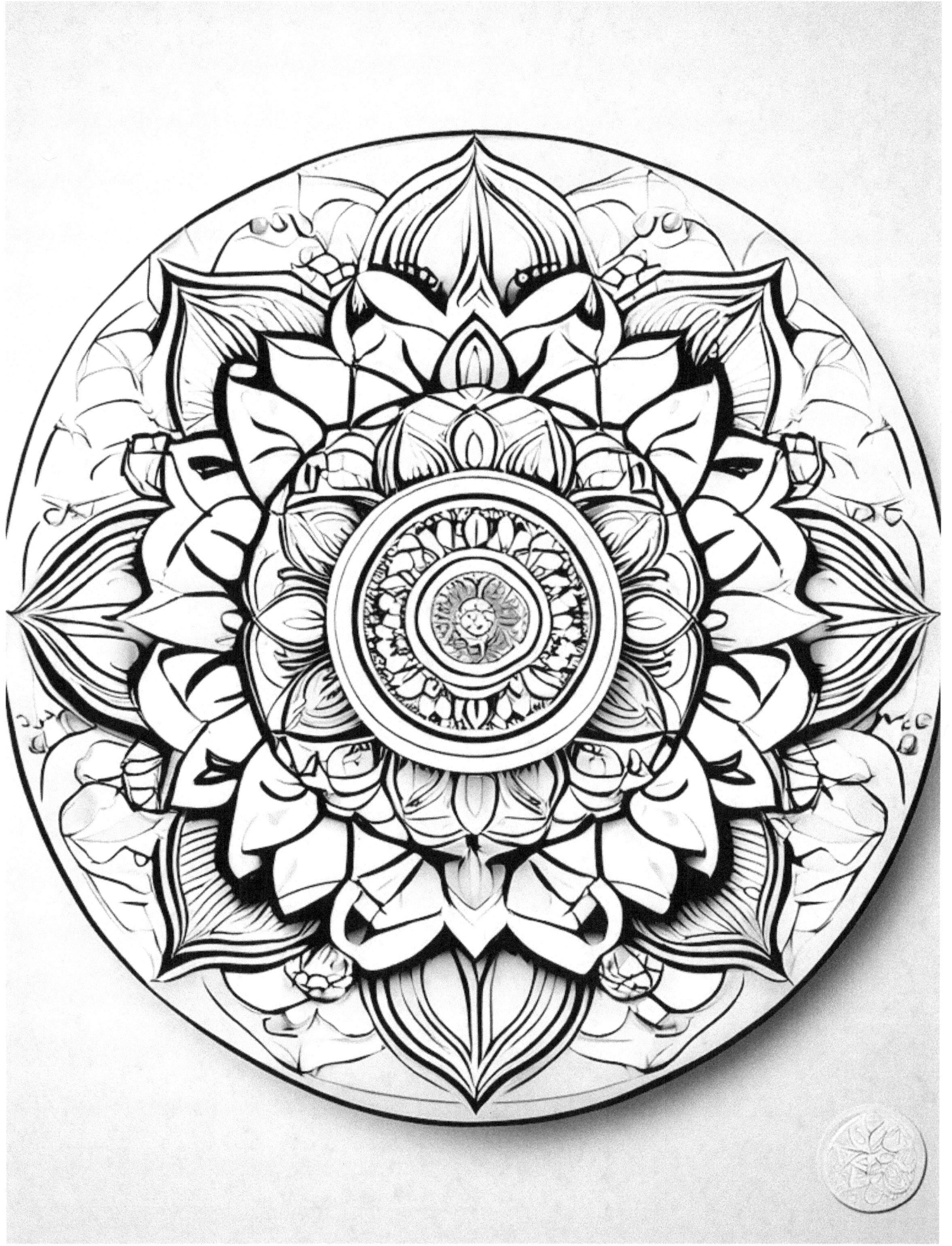

As you close this book, there comes to an end not only a coloring journey, but also an intimate journey towards your own inner peace.

May Zen Mandalas continue to inspire moments of serenity in your daily life.

Now, close your eyes for a moment, breathe deeply, and carry with you the sense of calm you found as you explored this book.

May your life continue to be an ever-evolving masterpiece, full of vibrant colors and harmonious patterns.

Until the next coloring journey, may it be filled with peace and inspiration.

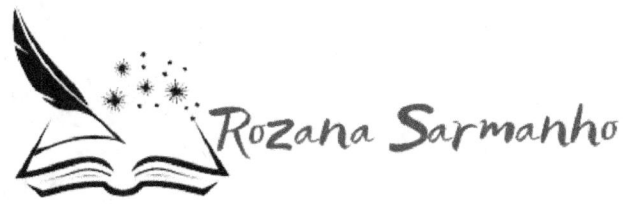

Rozana Sarmanho